BREATHING LIFE

PRANAYAMA YOGA TECHNIQUES

YOGI COUDOUX

Other books by Yogi Coudoux

Body Agreement (Corps Accord)

BREATHING LIFE

PRANAYAMA YOGA TECHNIQUES

YOGI COUDOUX

BREATHING LIFE

PRANAYAMA YOGA TECHNIQUES

Published in India by :
EMBASSY BOOK DISTRIBUTORS
120, Great Western Building,
Maharashtra Chamber of Commerce Lane,
Fort, Mumbai - 400 023.
Tel : (+91-22) 22819546 / 32967415
Email : info@embassybooks.in
Website: www.embassybooks.in

ISBN 13: 978-81-88452-37-8

Printed in India by Repro India Ltd.

TABLE OF CONTENTS

ILLUSTRATIONS

CHAPTER 1

The Opening of the Light

I want to offer you what has been given to me: to teach you to educate the body that has been given to you. I want to give you the means of finding within yourself, at every moment of your life, the breath of love that will build your strength, nourish your faith, and bolster your confidence. I want you to find the serenity you need so that your eyes express the sweetness of wisdom—the wisdom that comes from acceptance so that the light of God always shines on the roof of your house. I want to teach you to learn so that one day you, too, can send the sun to all those who approach you, and your body will reflect the joy and pleasure of living. This will permit you to awaken inside the hope that will unconsciously nourish your generosity and your ambitions so that, one day, life will allow you to be fully present and not simply exist. You will be spared much suffering.

These are three axes, all leading in the same direction: Time gives you patience, but you don't make use of it; life gives you peace, but you despise it; each second of your life shows you God, but you don't see Him. And yet, you are always seeking Him.

God has dispatched you into this world to find the light that leads to a unity of life that is indispensable in this quest to find the self. Who does not wish to feel a sense of freedom, well-being, and acceptance in the loving smiles of others?

Every day of my life, I close my eyes and gaze into the depths of my being in a prayer to the light. With all my love, I send a thought, an image to every thing that lives in this world. The coming together of life's movements can give each being the choice to follow the path towards the light with greater serenity, enriched by the tolerance that gives meaning to goodness.

I want every man, woman, and child, even those who are at the purely animal stage of their first life, to take the initial step towards listening to what they have, in order to find out who they are. My wish is to give each person the chance for well-being within his or her physical body and to help you acquire perfect knowledge of this vehicle that God has given you. That is what I want to give you, with all the strength my body transmits to me.

I speak to you in this manner so that each of my words creates an image within you, an image that leads you to meditation.

And, with all the greatness of love God has sent to me, I want you to learn to receive so that at any moment, you know how to breathe the breath of love, and you will be able to find the higher being that you are. When that happens, you can walk the path of communication, of listening, and of desiring to find your own body in order to understand it. Once you accept your body just as it is as the vehicle of your breath and soul, you can live in harmony with it and protect it better throughout your life.

I want to give you the means to receive sensations, a way of listening to the vibrations your body transmits that will help you open the door to your inner richness and accept each event in your life as a divine message you must translate. Use your body as a vehicle that travels the paths of life. Give your body what life gives to you: time—time to learn patience, to listen to what it has heard, to fix your gaze upon it, and to awaken all of its sleeping senses.

The person who remains satisfied with simply hearing what the body hears will never know how to listen, just as those who are satisfied with seeing with the body will never know how to gaze into the depths of what the eyes have seen or how to receive the messages sent for their highest and best good. But if you learn to gaze and to listen to your body properly, in order to interpret the life story that it sends you, then you will understand what love is. You will feel a great shiver running through all its form, giving birth to sensibility. You will translate this into a sweetness clothed in the colors of emotion. Your body will transmit this, just as purity calls forth innocence.

I want to lead you to the path of enlightenment. I want to

give you what has been given to me since the earliest days of my childhood: the pleasure of loving and the joy of giving in order to receive better.

I came into this world in Guadeloupe, a country whose beauty makes dragonflies sing. When my eyes viewed this spectacle, they admired the splendor of the wildflowers and the ballet of the coconut palms swaying to the movements of the generous winds. Every evening from my mother's house, located on the ocean's shore next to a river full of large-scaled fish, I could contemplate the sunset, which I called "the dance of the many-colored diamonds." Very often in the evening, the waves settled down and whispered softly in the wind. When the river lapped its banks and slid into the arms of the ocean with the complicity of the sky and hills, the marriage of fresh and salt waters made a thousand multi-colored petals appear. I used to spend hours watching this bed of diamonds in order to capture their forms and understand their meaning as they awakened my senses. These first images of my childhood softened the fibers of my heart, nourished my sensibility, aroused my emotions, and sharpened my curiosity.

One day at sunset, as my father and I sat on the bridge that crossed the river and splashed our feet in the cool, fresh water, we watched the golden sun in the distance as it slowly descended over the ocean. It lingered, as if regretting the fact that it was leaving. Little by little, as if to salute the sun, the sea calmed, changing its melody, and the song of the birds became louder. The seascape transformed from silver to gold passing through vermilion and gently gave birth to that heaven for the eyes and the breath, the ocean of petals.

After a while, I could no longer hear the water lapping against my father's feet. His eyes were closed, and his face tilted back slightly towards the sky, like a bird seeking to capture the echo of vibrations. His two hands were placed over each other, resting upon his thighs. I watched him for a few seconds before asking him, "Are you tired? Are you sleeping?"

He took some time to lower his head slowly to me, as if I had interrupted him. "No, I'm not sleeping, but I am listening to what I see so that I can inhale their vibrations better."

"But you can't listen to what you are looking at! And how do you breathe vibrations?" I exclaimed.

Instead of answering me, my father looked at me with those deep, gentle eyes that always reassured me so much. He let one hand caress the back of my neck briefly.

"Gaze at the water by your feet and tell me exactly what you see."

"Well, I see water, my feet, and the little fish. Oh, and I can see lots of stones moving down on the bottom."

"That's right. Except that the stones aren't really moving, but the movement of the water makes you think they are. Now, lift your head slightly to look a little farther in front of you. Try staring at the ripples in the water in order to see the little waves. Don't worry about the big ones, just the little ones.

Above all, don't sweep your eyes from right to left to look for them, because they're always wedded to the same spot. Relax your face as much as you can, especially your eyes, and let your body transmit all the love that's inside you."

"But how do you do that?" I asked.

"That's just what I'm starting to teach you. Breathe slowly and deeply. Each time you exhale, imagine that what you're exhaling is love that you're sending out. That's why you have to do it very gently, like a caress that you're giving to the ocean, to all these thousands of little waves that are sending colors to you. Pay attention: Each time you inhale, take the air in gently and deeply, as if you were receiving from all these petals the strength and the love they are giving you in return. Keep your face and your eyes relaxed the whole time, without trying to see the waves anymore, but try to penetrate them, to create an energy link between them and you. You will find strength there. Enfold them with your gaze, as if you were trying to protect them and to become just like them. You'll find love there."

"But how do I enfold them with my gaze?"

My father did not answer me with words but simply gave me a soft smile as he closed his eyes. Much later, I learned the meaning of his gesture. Then, my childish body was lacking in patience.

"Now that your eyes have seen the fish and your gaze has rested on them in order to join them to you better, try to relax your eyes even further. Imagine that your gaze takes the form of two big arms that wrap around your waves to protect them and that each time you take in air, you inhale. Also imagine you are hugging them to yourself, while listening happily to the melody of their movements, as if you were taking in deeply all the love they're returning to you. All the consideration you've transmitted to them has created this link between you, so the waves' vibrations have become fixed upon you and allow you to receive their echoes. You will experience this in the form of sensations that can be interpreted as revelations of love, as if your body were translating their movements to nourish sensations and visions of shapes within you. Close your eyes and point your chin in their direction. Let the images develop within you and gaze at what you have seen. Listen to what you have heard. You will find the vibrations, the echoes that will guide you into the depths of the forms you glimpsed just before.

"From now on, you will be able to find the depth of each movement in your breathing. This is the first key to the door leading to harmony. Each time you exhale, try to listen to what comes from you. Each time you inhale, open your doors wide, as if you were letting yourself be uplifted. Try to look, and you will find.

"What I've just explained to you is what I call 'gazing through existence.' I consider it indispensable to achieving any knowledge. I will teach it to you later, if you want."

My impatience crept in. "Oh yes, I want to learn this, but why later?"

"For me to explain it and teach it to you would be easy. It

would only take a few years. To understand and follow my teachings, however, will take your whole life. But I know you will succeed, because you have always been looking at these images without knowing it."

"What do you mean?"

"Remember all those times when you stared at something with a faraway gaze? That gaze gave the impression you were trying to form pictures to perfect your understanding and resolve some mystery. When your mother interrupted, asking, 'What are you thinking about?' you would almost always reply in a hesitant way, 'Nothing.' And then she said you were daydreaming. But really, without knowing it, you were simply gazing through existence. You were gazing at the forms that transmit vibrations, awakening sensations within you and plunging you into a state that took you away from the external world. That's why your mother asked, 'What are you thinking about?' instead of, 'Where are you?' And you didn't know the right answer yet, so you said, 'Nothing,' when you should have said, 'I'm gazing through existence, in order to better uplift myself.'"

In this way, my father explained that "gazing through existence" meant placing oneself in an internal state that allows communicating, sharing, and giving in order to receive better. It is a transfer of love and understanding between matter, movements, forms, and the vibrations that transmit their echoes. Even today, these early examples remain important basics for me.

"You see, at the beginning, when I asked you to gaze at

your feet, your answer showed you saw forms that seemed ordinary and unimportant to you, because you were content with merely seeing," he told me. "If you see a bird land on a branch near you and start hopping about, you might want to throw a pebble at it for fun. But if you take the trouble to observe it in order to appreciate its elegance, the brightness of its plumage, and the sweetness of its song, you will receive the echo of its vibrations, and you will begin to stop merely seeing it. That's the start of really looking, which I call 'gazing.' Instinctively, your face will grow softer, your eyes will light up, and little by little, your entire body will be filled with sweetness and peace—the communication of love. You will transmit a part of yourself to the bird so that you can receive from it better. You will create a link that facilitates gazing. It's the gaze that permits you to become part of the bird, while it becomes part of you. I call this link the you and your self.

"Once that link exists, you would no longer be able to harm the bird, because you have just finished bathing it with your gaze. In exchange, it has transmitted vibrations to you that permit you to feel the reflection of love. This short moment of happiness will remain engraved in you forever."

"I don't really understand what you call the 'you' and 'your self,'" I said.

"It's important for you to understand that the 'you' and 'your self' represent positive vibrations which reveal themselves more readily to those who take the time to gaze. The you is a thread that stretches out in order to be woven into your self.

It shows consideration and respect. Through the weaving, it transmits affection. It creates a link and becomes the cloth of purity for the dress that must cover and protect love. Its beauty nourishes positive vibrations.

"I am meeting most people who consult with me for the first time. And yet, I rarely address them formally. When I do so, it's because the images I receive of their mental state or their vibrations transmit scents that don't agree with me. So I address them formally, to keep them at a distance, far from my space, and to protect myself from their thoughts and their negative states. From their point of view, this may briefly diminish the amount of help they can expect from me. But later on, they will understand that I needed to give their bodies time to accept and grow accustomed to my way of being, which may seem very unusual and sometimes surprise even someone who has no preconceptions.

"Once their bodies have freed themselves from their unconscious anxieties and a sense of peace and security has been established, the doors that lead to their beings will quietly open wide, allowing me to give them freely the goodness they expect from me. Because even with the best will in the world, love and faith will never light up the inside of a house belonging to someone who obstinately keeps his doors locked."

This is how, while still very young, I understood that addressing someone informally is not a mark of disrespect or a lack of consideration, if you simply and sincerely want to give something to that person. It would be impossible for me to give you what has been given to me without love, consideration, and respect. That would mean betraying my father, my mother, and myself.

So, when I call you by your first name, I don't consider that as being overly friendly but as a means of joining with you. When I address you by your first name, it means my arms are wide open, and a place is reserved in my heart for you. It also means that I am ready to listen and give you what has been given to me, without holding back. It's slipping my hand into your hand in order to give you a part of myself in full complicity, like a breath of love or a sun that will always shine on the roof of your house.

I want to teach you how to look within in order to listen better, to bring you more awareness, and to awaken your sleeping senses. To stop being satisfied with just seeing. Above all, I would like to help you to stop simply existing within life, as though it were an endurance test. That is a mistake, an easy temptation that only engenders disappointment and suffering. It is running after time, instead of giving yourself time. It is cutting yourself off from all reality, from any real precision. I want to teach you, on the other hand, to breathe life in order to go and meet yourself.

You will need your body to reach the end of your path. Through it, you will find the inner light that will guide you to the self. You will always need this body as a guide to your inner state and to give it what you owe it: your protection and the love that will spill forth onto others. I want to teach you to accept your body as it is, whatever its external appearance.

You should never lose sight of the fact that denying, even unconsciously, the smallest part of your physical body will always make you feel ill at ease. This body is your house. Reign over it as its master, not as a slave to suffering and appearance. Don't force yourself to endure what others may try to impose, and don't allow them to interfere in the garden of your life without any thought for the disturbance they cause. Consider your body to be your one and only home, and your first reason for being, because it is your body that will show you the path. Consequently, guarding the quality of your life is your duty.

Let your mind visualize for a moment this unpleasant image: Would you allow a neighbor to dump his garbage in your living room? I want to teach you how to clean house inside, to breathe better so that you are inspired to live life fully. I want to teach you to learn to wait in order to find time and to teach your body the patience it lacks. As a result, you will be ready to harvest the breath of love that will allow you to restore harmony with your body, a body that will teach you to look and breathe with love.

To my way of thinking, any being is a child of God. Whatever our faith or religion—whether it is observed actively or passively, whether it is avowed or not—each of us can feel within ourselves the presence of God, either briefly or in a lasting way. Don't mistake my meaning when I say this, I can't force you to believe in God. These few lines would not be enough: To believe in something, you must first understand it and accept it. I just want to help you believe in yourself so that you can find your own path.

To say God doesn't exist is a right. You can permit this and be so persuaded for a large part of your life. This means you haven't yet found another person capable of finding the appropriate words to explain God concretely, although the image of God is abstract.

But one day you may feel an absolute need of divinity, even without daring to speak of it. And when you least expect it, you will encounter the person who knows how to listen before speaking and who will know how to gaze at you when expressing divinity. Little by little, a sensation of freedom will be born within you. A glow will take shape and develop day by day into a divine light that leads to God.

In reality, to look for God is the surest way to distance yourself from Him. To find the light that leads to God, the spark of the divine, you must start by seeking your Higher Self. Because we are all children of God, the light that leads to him lies within us. By finding that, you will find the path that leads to the unity of God.

If you satisfy yourself with merely living for the sake of daily existence, without seeking to find yourself or daring to speak of the divinity that awakens the sensibility and the emotion of love within you, you will never know the freedom that leads to supreme fulfillment or uplifting. Then, your physical life will have been devoid of meaning.

Your body is a vehicle you must protect; it also represents the house of your being. You must learn to arrange and shape it to be as inwardly perfect as possible. Always keep in mind, however, that in this world, perfection does not exist. This idea will permit you to find satisfaction that will nourish your morale. The more positive your beliefs, the more positive your morale will be. But be careful not to adopt images and thoughts that are conditioned by the views of others. You would surprise yourself by running into your own shadow and lose any sense of direction in your life.

In order to understand yourself better, try looking at what's around you and at your neighbors. Don't confuse seeing with gazing. Let your physical body, which is a real radar detector, receive and transmit the vibrations. Be attentive to the sensations that it communicates to you. Then you will understand that this animal body has a tendency to react spontaneously and to depend on the alertness of its senses.

This is the body's way of protecting itself. It is a normal self-defense process, but it distances you from reality and from your divinity. Be more attentive, and listen to your body more closely without imitating it. While the physical body simply reacts, you need to take more time before acting. Anyone who has received divine guidance should know that it is destined to be transmitted onward. The greatest riches will only be found once we understand that generosity doesn't lie in the hands of the one who gives but in the heart of the one who receives.

In the very instant when a recipient stretches a hand, with eyes closed, to take what is offered, that person's heart opens, the ego is repressed, and appearance is driven away. That person finds meaning wrapped in a robe of love, and develops a new outlook that will one day permit discovery of the Higher Self and lead to acceptance. For that person, life will be completely transformed.

The greatest force that can exist in this world is to be found where you least expect it—deep within you. That force forms part of your innate gifts, the automatic processes by which the body regulates itself spontaneously, according to its needs, without your being consciously aware of their nature, depth, and value.

I would like so much for you to take the time to find in my words the images you require for your meditation. That's why I offer you dozens of drawers filled with keys. You only need to learn how to use them in order to illuminate the path of meditation and open the doors that will lead you to the light. I want to teach you to listen to your body every second, to watch it move through the actions of its day and rest in the serenity of night. Because, even with the power of my love, I can only give you the keys. It is you who possesses the door; it is within you.

THE OPENING OF THE LIGHT

To find the keys to meditation, those that lead to acceptance, keep this book closed between both hands, horizontally, with

Opening of the Light

Figure 1

Figure 2

the open pages facing you (see figure 1). Isolate yourself from external influences by closing your eyes. Relax. Caress the book's front and back covers as you breathe deeply. Each time you inhale, concentrate on your own body, imagining that you are absorbing this book through the palms of your two hands. Each of the movements of your breathing should be filled with all your love. Upon exhaling, send along all the love and goodness you wish to communicate to those around you.

After three breaths, open the book to any page selected at random (see figure 2). Make yourself read only the second paragraph on the right-hand page. Read this in its entirety. Find the relationship between the text and you. It will be the key to your meditation.

In Buddha's spring, the child you are will be able to refresh itself while bathing in wisdom. This way of opening a book is called "Opening of the Light." In the morning, the message you get will enable you to understand, accept, and manage the events of your coming day better. In the evening, the message will help you visualize the events experienced during the day and prepare you for the meditation that will enrich your nighttime hours.

If you encounter a photo instead of words, it means you are trying to go too fast. You must learn to wait, to remain silent, and to listen in order to elevate yourself. However, you have the right to read the next paragraph. If you come upon another photo, you have reinforced the earlier message. That means you must really demonstrate wisdom and meditate on your actions in previous days in order to comprehend the days ahead better.

Another possibility is that opening the book leads you to purely technical explanations. This means you are undertaking, or are about to undertake, actions that require considerable reflection. You are on the right path in a difficult situation, but one that is less urgent than you think. In this case, continue reading until you come to the meditation key that will be the pillar of your strength. Give yourself time for meditation.

However, if your reading takes you to the following page, you should never continue reading as far as the next right-hand page. An opening that leads you to read that far means that you are about to begin a long-term task. Your patience needs to be reinforced. Or else, a change of direction is required.

Very often, you may keep opening to the same page. This indicates that the situation is delicate: Conditions are favorable, but you are unable to appreciate this. You're going around in circles and getting nowhere. Why? Because you dare not make the decisions that would allow you to advance out of fear of losing, of not being equipped for the task before you. You accept living without the ability to be your full self.

This is the only situation that permits you to close the book and start again. Still, you must take into account the significance of the first opening.

Perhaps you open to sentences that apply to your situation perfectly. You even think that it's not necessary to meditate. You are wrong. In this world, nothing is definitively acquired; you risk losing and becoming angry with yourself. You need to be more vigilant.

I hope you find the support for your meditation in this little saying that I've created for you: *He who runs after his shadow will run out of breath well before his physical body. It is preferable to sit in order to learn how to gaze.*

CHAPTER 2

The Language of Breathing

The first link in the chain of your life is breath. It supports and nourishes your life. However, the first form of nourishment for the body is love. In love, you will find the reason for your existence. But it is also love which will nourish your first mistakes and cause your greatest sufferings.

Material riches are only a means; they are ephemeral in nature. If you live in a world where material things are considered "wealth," know this is not true wealth and will never be. So, take care not to build on material things and never to make them the essential question. This does not prevent you from trying to create a life of maximum ease, but do so by working with respect, power, and conviction. If you provoke jealousy around you, you must remain creative and inventive.

Material wealth can turn out to be a means of helping you attain your goals while remaining in accord with the world in which you live. Make use of material wealth to nourish your ambitions and forge a will that is impervious to any ordeal, so that your energy can be nourished by it and never falter.

Don't let yourself be hindered by any obstacles that place

themselves in your path. On the other hand, accept the need to slow down when a situation arises that requires you to take time to understand and to find a way of crossing the mountain that rises before you. Give your body the patience that you must draw from time. Look and, in acceptance, you will find the reason that will support your strength.

Thanks to material wealth, many will come to you, and their eyes will reflect their pride in becoming your friend. Don't forget that those who really know how to measure the depth and value of friendship are rare. Give your confidence and esteem to those who do. In their presence, let your body express its sensitivity and generosity. Each time you find yourself alone, out of their physical presence, let their image and way of expression sweep across the screen of your memory and take time to look and listen to them. Meditate on these images. They will comprise the mirror in which you discover yourself. They will teach you that in order to understand yourself, you must learn to look at your neighbor.

Remind yourself that material wealth is only a means that may slip away from you tomorrow and that yesterday's friends may grow distant, forgetting even the fact of your existence. Don't get angry, don't despise them, and above all, don't judge them, because then you would blind yourself.

On the contrary, meditate on their ignorance in order to find within you the strength to understand errors. This will make you a stronger and more compassionate being tomorrow. Make use of these images to learn to look with serenity in the right direction to rediscover unity . . . the understanding of all things . . . the unity of life. These will be keys of meditation for you. Above all, don't let them fly away, like stray thoughts carried off by a raging sea, without ever reaching safe port.

You are not in this world so that life can make use of you but so that you can make use of living through the intermediary of your life. What are we all trying to see, feel, hear, listen for, breathe, and even inspire, like an essence that awakens our senses, even if we don't admit it? Love! Once you transmit love, you rediscover the most beautiful colors and vibrations that envelop love and awaken generosity within you.

Sensitivity is the color of the clothing love wears. It is an infinite vibration of the divine that nourishes your being. It caresses your body like an alloy of hot and cold air currents that merge in order to awaken awareness of your body's patterns. It is like a kiss that may make you blush or shiver, dilating your arteries and all the pores of your skin, in order to guide you toward hearing the splendor of your divinity. Sensitivity is part of your strength; it is at your disposal to uplift you. It is your duty to make use of it. Consequently, you must learn to breathe sensitivity, so that your body can transmit it through all the pores of your skin. Your sensitivity is an asset that can lead you to the true revelation of the divine essence—a power to show you the path of tolerance and goodness and help you find the switch that will put you in the light of your Higher Self.

However, instead of attaching proper value to it, you commit the error of seeing your sensitivity as a sign of weakness. This ignorance will bring suffering. You will often feel ill at ease, in a position of inferiority before others, and your self-esteem will be severely reduced.

You have no right to feel this way! Starting today, consider your sensitivity as a force of liberty and of reality. Let it come forth; don't hold back. Let it dance with your senses. Play with it and explore it like a curious and amused child. Take the time to discover its vibration within you.

Take care never to confuse sensitivity and emotional expression. If the former lends its colors to love, the latter represents the fabric of its dress. It will envelop you each time your heart lays itself bare. Emotional expression upsets the rhythm of your body's life and makes you feel the beating of your heart, like the hooves of a frightened horse during a wild gallop. It will make you vibrate to the point of provoking inexplicable sobs of joy that will free your body from its restraints. It will bring forth purifying tears, shining with the light of your inner self.

Emotional expression is a gift from God. Its role is to awaken you to the path of awareness, to show you the disposition of what should emanate from your body. You need to listen to this in order to protect your body. With the very first vibrations of emotion, sensitivity will spill forth from its breast. This is how you will take your first steps towards divinity.

Starting today, let this force born of love emanate freely from your body in order to spark the light of your sensitivity. You will find acceptance and tolerance in the gazes of all those who are fortunate enough to meet you. The body that radiates sensitivity automatically awakens the image of sweetness within those who look upon it. The body becomes imbibed with one of the most beautiful colors in life, a reflection of the sweetness that comes from love, the principal source of existence. Sensitivity is like a lover; it attracts others like buzzing bees are attracted to pollen.

You will be making a grave error if you stubbornly refuse to listen to the voices of emotion and sensitivity. Your body will then depend solely on appearance, on the images you receive from others or those emitted by people who judge you. You will be guided by the negative thoughts you read into another's gaze, and you will make of yourself what you believe others think of you.

Make the decision to repair this error without hesitation, rather than unwittingly destroying yourself. Submit to your sensitivity and your emotional voices.

Sensitivity is the path of light that leads to God. Emotional expression is the sign that marks the route. These few words bring forth memories of myself as a small boy, caressed by the first rays of the sun. Coming home from school on my eighth birthday, I told my father about the difficulties I had in understanding the behavior of my fellow classmates, who persisted in hitting me for no reason other than the pretext that I was afraid to get into fights.

I must admit that sensitivity has always emanated freely from me. For someone who sees but does not know how to gaze, it is easy to confuse this with weakness. Like them, I became lost in this confusion little by little, to the extent of becoming incapable of finding my place or accepting myself. This was a very negative period for me. I had never known aggressiveness before. I had no wish to do physical or moral harm to those whose friendship I desired so much.

I always took great pleasure in confiding in my father. He took the time to listen to me and found the right words to help me communicate the images in my mind. For long hours I explained my despair to him, asking, "Why don't they want me as a friend? Why do they hit me for no reason? Why do they think I'm cowardly and weak? Why do I feel so bad?"

At that time, I got no answers to all these questions, which were filled with the pain that vibrated in my little boy's body. At least, that was how it seemed to my eight-year-old reasoning.

My father gazed at me tenderly. We were sitting under an avocado tree, just in front of our house. He got up without a word and took me by the hand.

I followed him into the house, where he pointed to an ancient cloth-covered book. I took it as he asked me to, and we returned to sit under the avocado tree. This time, we were face-to-face.

"Contrary to what you believe, what you just told me is nothing negative. The negative does not exist. Don't believe for a single instant that you belong among the cowards and weaklings. You must never forget that, if you only look at your reflection in the eyes of others, you will always be what you believe others think of you.

"These encounters are just signs of the progress in your education. If they arouse suffering or bad feelings in you, it is simply to bring you toward meditation. That is why I haven't answered your questions. The answers lie within you, but you must find the path that will lead you to them. It's by following this path that you will grow up."

My father took the book from my hands, placed it upon his crossed legs, and read some lines to himself. Then, gently, he closed the book before placing it once again between my hands. "You see, this book is many centuries old; it is the sacred book of Buddha's teachings." That is how I started to learn the Opening of the Light—my first steps towards meditation.

At school the next day, the little boy had grown up. I no longer sought to become the friend of others at any price; paradoxically, friends came to me. That day has remained one of the most rewarding of my life.

Although I have trained numerous yoga teachers throughout the world, I have never given as much as I am now. Through this writing, I am asking you to walk a few steps with me so that you can feel my constant presence at your side, guiding you on your path. This will permit you to meet the father I have known, to awaken and nourish within you the strength you need, to teach you to recognize that strength in all its forms, to avoid mistaking one form for another, and to accept all of these truths in order to grow.

The more you give, the more you will find confidence. Then, one will read purity in your eyes.

Help your body walk beside you, hand in hand. Help your body free itself from preconceptions, and you will find freedom and fulfillment. This will make you a well-disposed being in a body that is at your command.

I want to give you the means of finding confidence in yourself under any circumstances. There will be no more question of letting yourself be imposed upon, of letting others do violence to you without understanding why. You are in this world in order to learn, but circumstances do not always give you the possibility of finding within you images that are strong enough to nourish your determination and perseverance.

In practice, life provides everything you need to find the path of serenity that raises your perceptions and your choices and leads to uplifting. However, you have not yet been taught to look at "the" life or to listen to the messages transmitted by the vibrations of your own body that give witness to your existence and the activity of "your" life.

It is essential for you to acquire the sense of desire that generates motivation. This is indispensable for building courage, which provides further nourishment to your morale so that you get closer to your goal every day. Without wanting to achieve, grow, or acquire something, you will be lacking in will.

The basis of all this is learning to communicate with your body and listening to it as you move through this world. It must never again be a stranger to you. Everything your body does, you must do with it, in total complicity. Learn to understand it. You are in a body for that purpose. It is the path, the light that leads to knowledge. It is the means of achieving your purpose on this planet.

Without your body, nothing is possible—but that is still not saying enough to express this idea. One would almost have to invent a new expression: *Without the body, everything is impossible.*

Breathing is a real science, the science of living—and of living in good health. Just because the body breathes automatically and performs this movement spontaneously, without even the aid of the conscious mind, does not mean that it isn't necessary to teach the body how to breathe. To neglect learning to breathe is extremely serious.

Give breathing the primary importance it deserves. The duration and the quality of your life depend on it. Whether you are in a polluted place or the high mountains, your respiration will adapt, and your cardiac rhythms will accelerate to seek more oxygen, or conversely, slow down. It is not a question of trying to prevent these modifications, which are strictly independent of your will. However, you can learn to help your body improve them in order to make its life easier.

Before attempting any breathing exercises, it is crucial to give you the reasons for undertaking them. How many times, just when you were ready to give the best of yourself—for an exam or an important interview, for example—have you found yourself in a situation where you lost your serenity and your faculties? You were unable to fulfill your potential. Afterwards, you looked back with regret as you saw your errors scrolling down the screen of your memory. And you wanted another chance.

The reason for your failure lay where you least suspected it. Because of that, you run the risk of letting yourself be surprised again in the future, of reproducing the same scenario, and of repeating the same situation indefinitely.

I intend to give you the way out of this spiral of failure so that you never lose the possibilities in any important situation. It's up to you to give yourself the time to learn and understand these methods, in order to put them into practice fully.

Don't think that all you have to do is snap your fingers; things won't start happening instantly. Your body must understand what you expect of it in order to accept and adopt these and other automatic responses. You will have to solicit your body's participation through daily training.

Your breathing modifies itself hundreds of times each day, without your being aware of it. It is constantly modifying your bodily functions, nourishing and supporting your life, which depends upon it. It feeds the chain of life, of which it constitutes the first link. It is both the beginning and the end of that chain. It would be unthinkable for the education of your body not to begin by the study of the breath. You should not forget for even an instant to teach it to breathe better in order to exist more freely. Learning to breathe will permit you to discover your physical body fully, to preserve its health, and give you and ease of living that's invaluable. The most extraordinary thing of all is that, by arousing such cooperation with your physical body, you will further awaken that intuitive or (invisible) part of yourself that absorbs and interprets the world and its images—your mental body.

TELL ME HOW YOU BREATHE

In everyday life, breathing takes place automatically through the rear of the nose. The process of inhalation should last about two seconds, followed by a pause of a second leading to the switchover to exhalation, which should go on for about two and a half seconds. A second pause of about two seconds establishes the balance of the movement in its continuity.

How many times in your daily life has poor management of your breathing become your own worst enemy, provoking nervous states that ruined what should have been glorious, unforgettable moments? When nervousness takes over, the rules of breathing are abandoned. The process accelerates and becomes disjointed. Your hands grow damp, and sweat appears at various points of the body as modifications of the normal bodily functions take place. Once you become aware of this state, your mind becomes your enemy. Words fail you,

you lose your faculties, and you are unable to recover the assurance you possessed only a moment before. You have just destroyed an important moment in your life due to simple ignorance of your inner resources.

To prevent this condition from recurring and to remain calm and serene under any circumstance, you need to learn how to breathe in a way that maintains total control over your body. In this particular case, the process of exhalation will become important. Keep your mind focused on each aspect of the process in order to relax your face as much as possible. The body is a radar detector that picks up external stimulation and transmits it mainly through the face. Once you have focused your mind on relaxing the facial muscles and on the regularity of the movements of exhalation, the entire body will follow and progressively loosen up.

Visualize this search for relaxation descending, little by little, towards the solar plexus and the belly. Make the exhalation deep enough and long enough to allow time for the relaxation to run the full course.

I want to lead you to control your body, to reach a state of complete harmony so that you will at last appreciate your life as you deserve. Learn to look at your body, to let it breathe with love in order to find within it the splendor of life—your path. This path will give greater scope to the confidence being born within you. You will possess greater strength to sweep obstacles aside. You will give yourself the means to rise above suffering and maintain control over your reactions without letting yourself be surprised by anxiety or fear of failure when faced with an important matter.

This exercise is much easier than it seems. Start today: Prepare your body to become your ally.

Let's look at some specific situations in order to understand this exercise and put it into concrete practice better.

Situation 1: Meeting Someone Face-to-Face

Breathe very deeply and make sure that each movement of exhalation is naturally slow and deep. At the same time, try to relax your face and belly as much as possible. The relaxation of the belly is crucial. With practice, your face will reflect this calm and serenity.

This exercise is aimed at protecting the body from external aggression, as well as nervous and muscular tension. At the beginning, you may feel a sense of fatigue that will even provoke yawning. In reality, your body is releasing its tiredness by eliminating accumulated stress and undesirable tension. To aid it further, it would even be desirable to accentuate the yawns and accompany them by improvising stretching movements, remembering to keep your facial muscles relaxed at the same time. You will feel an intense regeneration, like a new birth. After taking five breaths, you will feel a state of loosening up, of peace and well-being.

Your body will transmit the peace that will be settling within it. Your relationship with the person in your life at that moment will benefit from this serenity. By seeking out the mind's cooperation and keeping it focused on exhalation and relaxation, you don't allow it time to be invaded by vibrations external to your own vital movement. Your body will ignore the panic that previously scrambled your faculties.

Here is another practical example that follows the technique I have just given you. It is also easy to understand, learn, and put into practice.

Situation 2: An Important Meeting, Exam, or Interview

As you approach the place where you have an appointment, take care not to make any brusque or jerky movements. Begin by repeating the technique described in the first situation. Let your body emanate peace, assurance, tranquility, precision, and generosity.

Now, anchor in your memory this fond image that must remain constantly present: Think of your body as a person dear to you that you want to protect with all the strength of your affection, as though it were a suit of armor that would deflect any unconscious projections of aggression that could upset it. Do this because the person you meet instinctively interprets any jerky movement in a negative fashion, which could be to your disadvantage.

Don't ever stop breathing deeply. But, of course, don't let anyone hear or see these breaths. When walking, count a given number of steps for each inhalation. Your pause in breathing, with lungs full, should last one-quarter of this time. When exhaling, you should increase the number of steps by one-quarter.

The movements of your breathing will instinctively

become caresses which envelop your body in the cocoon of love. Your essential being is love; it protects your body. It will no longer need you to interpret each inhalation as kisses that awaken its charms, illuminating its life with the flash of goodness that it will transmit.

When exhalation occurs, try to relax your face and belly so that your body can receive this exhalation like a caress. It will make your body melt in the tenderness of your gaze and merge with you. The process of exhalation will be slower and consequently longer that that of inhaling, but do not exhale more air than you've taken in.

Here is an example of a complete deep breath count:

- Eight steps during inhalation
- Two steps during the pause with full lungs
- Ten steps during exhalation
- Two steps during the pause with empty lungs

Before you really learn how to breathe, you won't have sufficient respiratory capacity to achieve this count without running out of breath. For the moment, just take it as an example and adapt it to your own level, without ever forgetting to keep the image described above in your mind.

Don't wait until you have an important meeting. Start the education of your body today, but don't rush into it before you have understood the steps and the purpose. Finish what you have started; don't be content with short little attempts that won't get you anywhere.

You are learning to breathe in order to help your body live better. You won't run out of breath with the slightest effort, smoke because other people do, get irritated over nothing, or punish yourself and those who are dear to you. Learn to breathe so that you no longer take that bumpy road of anger that leaves your body with wounds bathed in regrets, upsetting your ego to the point that you grow distant from sincerity. Learn to breathe so that your body finds a peaceful and restorative sleep whenever it needs it, and so you are rid of any bad feelings.

Breathe the happiness of being and of living serenely. Aren't those really good reasons?

Situation 3: The Language of the Yogi, or the Language of Breathing

Suppose you are face-to-face with someone who is going to judge your worth or expects something from you that you consider important. From the first moment, take care not to speak with automatic, uncontrolled breaths. Always breathe deeply, your inhalations arriving through the rear of your nose and your exhalations departing from the back of your throat. Let your breath exit from your mouth; make use of this prolonged exhalation to form your sentences. Shape each of your words with your breath. Use the process of exhalation and the relaxation of your belly to build the volume of your voice. (However, you should know that in order to emit a word you also have to shape the vocal cords. This requires daily training so that your body inscribes it into its automatic responses.)

At the end of each sentence, take the time to close your mouth. Indicate a pause. Make sure your belly is loosened up before inhaling through your nose. The length of the pause will lend weight to your sentence and will complete it or leave the next moment in suspense.

You should concentrate on avoiding a high-pitched voice and favor lower or medium tones. Your voice should attain a good range while keeping its character. The push of each exhalation should come from the belly, with the rhythm and movements of your words, retracting the diaphragmatic muscles and contracting the viscera as slowly as necessary. Train your mind to focus on ventral relaxation during the process so that your physical being finds the peace it often lacks. At the same time, educate your mind to collaborate perfectly with your physical being, thus permitting you to control the ventral movements better while speaking. Little by little, you will obtain the harmony that will generate the greatest energy in your life.

This breathing technique requires you to speak calmly and transmit the peace that emanates from you to the person who's listening. Picture your breath as a caress of love that you are sending to the other person. Without realizing it, the other person's body will interpret it as such. You will open up within that person the path of communication that encourages listening and sharing.

Thanks to this technique, you will begin to develop innate talents that have been dormant for a long time. It will be fantastic to surprise yourself as you become familiar with your body. Your happiness will be great!

To help your body transmit and receive vibrations more easily, it is vital to keep the facial muscles relaxed. This will prevent the person with whom you are dealing from setting up an automatic system of physical self-defense—the natural, spontaneous reaction of any animal body protecting itself from external aggression. Fill your gaze with a smile of love and acceptance that will be interpreted by the other as a message of goodness and generosity. As your mouth opens to utter a word, imagine a note or a sound that naturally requires you to relax your vocal cords as your throat widens. Then imagine the beginning of a generous smile that envelops the other person, like the curves of the ocean's movements that sing with the wind and form a wave. At the end of your exhalation, your sentence will be incomplete if it ends on the crest of the wave. If it ends in the hollow of your throat, it will give birth to a period.

Now take your time to inhale deeply through the nostrils. It is assumed that the process of exhalation is ventral. Concentrate on never starting in a high-pitched voice. This will unconsciously increase others' nervous tension and arouse their defenses. To do this while speaking, watch that the throat muscles and vocal chords stay relaxed.

During your interview, never let your gaze wander off to what surrounds you. Subconsciously, the other person will interpret that as a lack of interest. That would risk negative vibrations that cause your interview to fall short of its goal and hinder any opening towards a real connection. Don't forget that the physical body is also nourished by vibrations that it interprets automatically, without involving the mind. Always express your feelings in the way you look at the other person.

Look into the other person's eyes, which will express the importance you attach to the words being spoken. Also look into the region of the solar plexus, so that the other's body can interpret the depth to which you are pondering the spoken sentences.

Never lower your head for more than three seconds. The other person will subconsciously interpret that as a refusal to communicate out of fear or submission.

More than anything, I hope to help you find the path that will permit you discover your self and to believe in yourself so that your body finds the confidence and freedom that will facilitate your life.

I want you to learn the confidence that you are lacking so badly. For that to happen, you must learn to become a child of God once again, to become love. Teach your body to transmit love with purity and sincerity. If your physical being naturally tends towards aggressiveness, it does so out of its constant state of self-defense. You must help it eliminate this aggressiveness and feed it with love and loving actions, which transmit goodness, acceptance, and tolerance.

Above all, make sure that your body never expresses arrogance. One who speaks little arouses interest and curiosity in the other person. To permit your body to express your confidence and sincerity and to permit the other person to receive them, so that the person will believe in you, you must absolutely believe in yourself.

Your faith will be your strength. This strength will transmit the light that will give the other person the desire, and even the need, to look and listen to you. That person's gaze upon you will nourish your confidence. Both of you will be protected by this great veil of tolerance and fraternity.

The steps you must accomplish on this path belong to you. You are the sole master of your wants and your efforts. However, to teach you to advance correctly on your path, I will take you by the hand. To give you greater assurance and settle you in a sense of security, I will walk by your side. If you were alone with my words, your body would risk racing against time in order to attain the desired result too quickly. That would allow the garden of your life to be invaded by three devastating weeds—impatience, doubt, and nervousness.

I want to help you become a good gardener so that you can cultivate the tree of your life and pick and appreciate its fruits. But above all, I want you to love the garden of life that surrounds you and to respect the earth as one respects the source of your life's purpose, without which you will never have the knowledge that leads to supreme fulfillment and uplifting.

Like the earth, your body breathes. That is the first link in the chain of its life. To begin the education of your body, you must learn breathing—by which everything commences and everything ends. By controlling the breath, you will succeed in your approach and obtain what you want. You will become a true gardener of life.

I have just given you some useful tools for building self-confidence. Now, you must practice. Training is indispensable as your body adapts to its new life and constantly solicits the cooperation of the mind and the plan of the conscience. These are the partners that share the tasks leading to satisfaction.

Each day of your life, your body receives hundreds of aggressive impulses and sensations. The conscience doesn't give the mind time to act on them. Your physical being reacts by contracting, accumulating nervous tension, modifying its blood pressure, and creating imbalances in your blood platelets. The list is much longer and only concerns the physical body, the grossest manifestation of being.

The mind, which is mixed up with the physical being, builds up a sense of malaise through thousands of images and stray thoughts, many of them unconscious. Thus are born the first forms of anxiety that will develop day after day.

Your body grows inebriated with tiredness and does not give you the choice of stopping to rest. Like a swimmer who drowns in a general fatigue, you lose your footing in the basin of depression. You are afraid of being misunderstood.

Starting today, you will begin to learn to protect your body from any external aggression and even the antidote to its own spontaneous reactions, thus achieving freedom and fulfillment.

Above all, you will find within yourself the reason that gives birth to your desire to undertake this. *Like a child dazzled by the image of the life it is discovering, you will grow up to understand.*

CHAPTER 3

Wipe Out the Negative

To understand the great richness of breathing, it's important to listen to your body. Your body produces between ten and forty inhalations per minute, or an average of 36,000 per day. It takes in between 780 and 900 cubic feet of air per day, which acts on your internal balance.

You have probably never really paid attention to this—and yet, your whole life depends on it! Does your life matter so little to you that you won't even bother to educate your body's breathing in order to utilize it properly? Listen to your body so that you can meet life.

Asana is the sanskrit word for "posture." In this section, you will be introduced to some asanas that will give you a foundation for listening to your body. These asanas will help you learn to breathe.

Learning to breathe does not mean imposing detrimental obligations or tensions on the body. To learn how to breathe, discover your body, receive its vibrations, and listen to its echoes. This will start you off. Without practicing such awareness, all your seeking will be in vain, whether it involves concentration, relaxation, or meditation. After you determine why you are taking the steps to breathe greater life into your body, you will find "the willpower that is born of wanting." You will become a willing accomplice with your body. You will know the pleasure of breathing in a loving way.

Close your eyes to remove yourself from external influences. Isolate yourself in the respiratory movements of your body, a melody that will grow in strength and reveal its state to you. Upon inhaling, receive these vibrations like a gentle kiss that draws you in and transports you toward a weightless body state. Finish your inhalation like the end of a tender and subtle kiss from a loved one. During the pause that follows, listen to your body, go towards it, and breathe into it.

Exhalation is the moment when your body comes to you like the smile of a child filled with wonder who discovers, for the first time, the features of a person whose voice is already familiar. Receive this smile, the echo of your body, like a thin veil that floats in your internal space. It descends to the core of your being to awaken your Higher Self. It joins with your body so that you may find your path. In the landscape of your life, learn to watch the wind of exhalation and listen to the echoes it transmits. Those echoes will guide you to your path.

To perform any exercise correctly on the path of yoga and Buddhism, you need to clothe yourself in appropriate attire, establish a training regimen, and pick a tranquil place where you cannot be disturbed.

THE ATTIRE (FOR BOTH MEN AND WOMEN)

Clothing facilitates awakening by putting you in the right frame of mind so that your mental body encompasses your physical body, and they may integrate you in creating the serenity that will illuminate your house. To obtain more from your body than automatic reactions that only result in spontaneous gymnastic motions, you need to clothe it just as the Yogi does. Thanks to wearing this attire, your body will transmit sensations that will improve your attitude.

The clothing recommended for your yoga practice includes:

- A "seeker's loincloth," reserved for the daily asanas;
- A "smaller loincloth of light," for meditation;
- A kimono.

The seeker's loincloth is a piece of cotton or silk cloth, two yards long and one yard wide. The narrower loincloth of light should measure three yards long and one foot wide. Over your loincloth, if necessary, you may wear a kimono made of silk or cotton. The belt for the kimono goes twice around the waist. It is four to six inches wide and three yards long. For women, it is tied on the left; for men, on the right.

THE TRAINING

It would be a pity and not very interesting to treat your asanas as gymnastics, because you would never have the opportunity to discover your inner space and richness. Your body needs more training day after day, in order to become accustomed to the movements and find the comfort that provides ease.

It is vital for your body to adapt and adopt what you ask of it as part of its automatic responses, integrating the movements into the automatic cycle that comes with habit. After that, the brain will no longer need to ask the mental body to interpret the movements to be performed. They will be registered in the automatic responses; one will lead automatically to the next. Consequently, the mental body will have no difficulty in presenting you one of its "children," an image that will become your ally in the necessary moment. It will draw all of the sensations and impressions felt by the physical body and interpreted by the mental body. The mental body will provide the meaning of these experiences and transmit the images to your inner focus. After that, it will it possible for you to close your eyes, imagine, and find. Henceforth, the level of the image will always be available to permit you to listen to the feelings of your body and facilitate their comprehension.

Your goal is to find within yourself the force born of faith and willpower—itself the child of desire. Don't content yourself with seeing the point of energy. Gaze upon it so that your inner focus blends in and harmonizes with your breathing, because each inhalation will make it deeper and more penetrating. You will breathe this inner gaze that transmits energy. You will absorb energy and become energy. You will make use of the image to consider the point of light as a source of energy. Its role is to fill your body with power and to unite you with it.

THE PLACE

Since this attention to listening is the start of your body's education, you must not neglect anything. You owe it to yourself to be attentive to the slightest reaction or sensation of your body, which must constantly feel that you are not only listening to it, but also taking care of it. Enable it to feel and become reacquainted with the peace that will lead you to serenity and well-being. Your body is vital to the success of your search, but the place you exercise is also important, because it transmits many vibrations.

The religious man takes up residence in a house that may seem ordinary before it is devoted to a spiritual calling. Entering this place, he will draw from within himself the peace he requires for prayer. He will always take care to speak softly to allow his body the time to transmit the respect and consideration which will impregnate this place. The vibrations of his faith will radiate all around his body to inhabit this dwelling little by little, enveloping it completely with his conviction. He will build the soul of his residence with his prayers. This place will become sacred. It will be his temple, his church. Anyone who enters will sense the peace and generosity that emanate from the place, and they will give it their respect, thereby modifying their behavior.

You have chosen your place of exercise. Is the place you have chosen inside or outside? Obtain a fairly thick mat for your sessions. Avoid direct contact with concrete or synthetics, and always protect yourself with your mat. Give preference to outside locations whenever possible.

Asana of Liberation

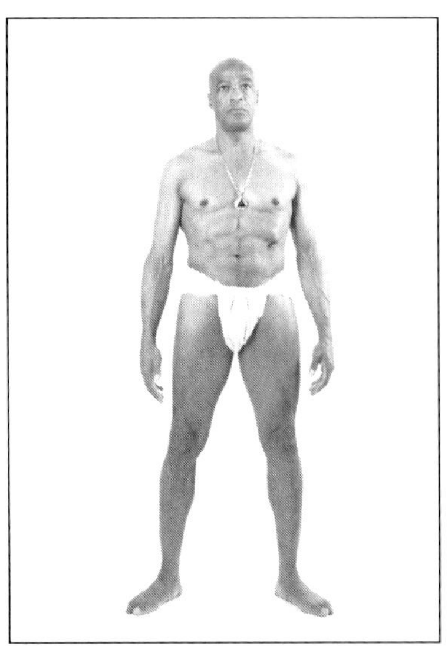

Figure 3

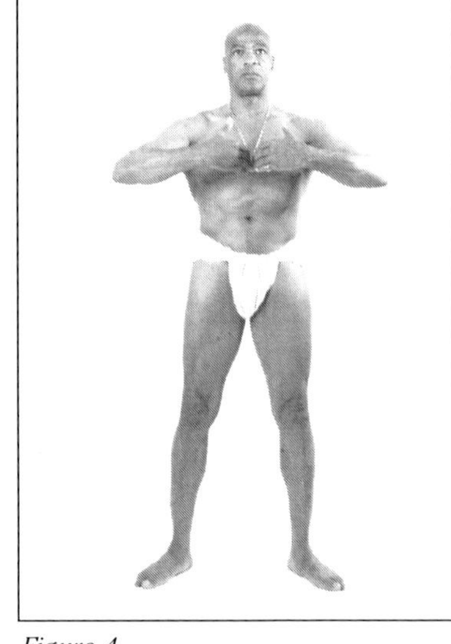

Figure 4

Figure 5

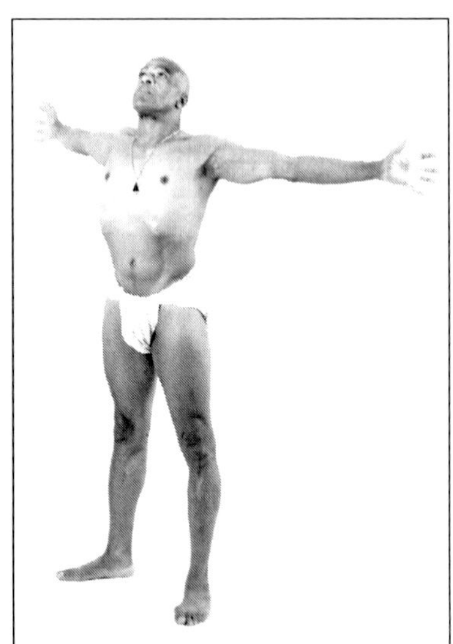

Figure 6

You also need to organize yourself so that your space only offers positive vibrations. To do that, you must bring harmony to this place and provide it with the passion of your soul.

To encourage benevolent vibrations, always point your face towards the east, south, or west. Avoid facing north. Consider your body an individual to whom you are transmitting the full depth of your love. Avoid practicing in the presence of any person who is not engaged in the same type of spiritual seeking as yourself.

Like the religious man, you will make your body what it really is—your dwelling. You will enhance its virtues and confirm that it is the temple of love. Your body will then be your church. To meet your self, this is the path you must follow. If you accept this education and apply it to your life, you will become a child of the spring of Buddha. The reasons of wisdom will always guide your steps. Upon your road, the light will always be present, and in your eyes, the colors of love will flower forever.

THE ASANA OF LIBERATION

Let us begin with the technique for free breathing, the Asana of Liberation. This asana will help you realize the influence of breathing over your body and lead your body towards well-being. Proceed according to these steps:

• Stand with your legs straight. The distance between your feet should correspond to the width of your shoulders (see figure 3).

• Relax your arms at the sides of your body, shaking them in order to loosen them fully.

• Regardless of the current depth of your breathing, sigh deeply three times. This enables your body to understand that you are eliciting its cooperation to create a state of well-being. Throughout your exhalations, relax the muscles of your face as much as possible. Let the rest of your body settle into this relaxation.

• Lift your arms in front of you and place your hands back-to-back, drawing your fingers into the solar plexus (see figure 4).

• Raise your elbows, shift your shoulders forward, and tip your pelvis slightly backwards to give yourself a rounded back, like a cat when it stretches (see figure 5). You will feel this stretching along the dorsal section of your spinal column (opposite the heart).

• Inhale deeply and strongly through the rear of your nose. Open your arms wide to form a semicircle in front of you. Imagine that you are opening window shutters in your house.

• Shift your arms backwards to stretch yourself. At the same time, tip your pelvis forward. Your arms should remain level with the height of your shoulders (see figure 6).

• Spread all your fingers very wide and bend them slightly, like claws, to create a complete stretch right to your fingertips.

• While maintaining this position, inhale and stretch your entire body. Pause to feel the tension draining from it.

• Before exhaling, release your arms to the sides of your body. Let your head fall forward, then exhale deeply from the back of the throat.

• During exhalation, relax your throat enough to make the

vocal cords vibrate in a sound similar to a sigh of satisfaction.

• Don't forget to relax your entire body during exhalation.

Take note of these points:

• During inhalation, seek power, volume, and length. Your inhalation should produce a sound similar to wind whistling through the sails of a ship.

• Throughout your stretching, never stop inhaling. Even when your lungs seem full, keep inhaling, as if the pause after the inhalation does not exist.

• Before exhaling and as you relax, release your arms to the sides of your body. Let your head fall freely and effortlessly forward, like a rag doll's. The weight of your head should stretch the muscle cords of the cervical vertebrae, which will relax naturally.

• When exhaling, imagine the gentle waves of the ocean that come to caress the pebbles on the beach or a long, moaning sigh that indicates the enjoyment of well-being.

• To perform one round of the Asana of Liberation, inhale for three seconds, stretch and pause for six seconds, exhale for three seconds, and pause between breaths for three seconds.

From the very first asana you perform, your face will want to relax and feel the sweetness that caresses it. Your body will speak to you. It's up to you to listen and breathe in this feeling to affirm your love for your body.

Repeat the Asana of Liberation with free breathing at least

five times to give your body the sense of well-being it seeks. This simple asana will give you the comfort and pleasure of living freely with your body. Learn to listen to your body and its feelings and to control them.

When to Perform this Asana

The Asana of Liberation can be performed at any hour of the day. For the sake of your body, put the Asana of Liberation into practice anytime you feel the need. For example, do the Asana of Liberation when you're nervous or when fear heightens the anxiety inside your body. When troubled by incomprehensible messages, your frightened body tends to lose its bearings, and fatigue can lead you astray from familiar points of reference. Also, do this asana when you have a desire to feel the blossoming of your body's naturally expansive, cooperative state.

When you feel that your body needs you, stop everything—regardless of the place, moment, or reason that occupies your time. Be there for it. Make a conscious effort to give your body what belongs to you—time.

You can perform this exercise when your body is tired or your back aches. Two or three asanas will be enough to rebalance the energy in your body and erase minor pains and fatigue while restoring your morale to a positive place.

When practiced on its own, the Asana of Liberation is ideally a morning asana. Create a daily routine without getting ahead of your abilities. You have all the time you need. Practice this asana once a day for at least five minutes.

At the end of the week, you will start to feel a greater sense of well-being.

Another time to perform the Asana of Liberation is at the start of each session. It will prepare your physical and mental bodies so that you can obtain the most responsive results from them.

This asana is indispensable at the end of each session. You should also perform it in the middle of your sessions and anytime you feel the body is out of breath or tense.

Avoid rushing into any other asanas before fully learning and integrating the Asana of Liberation, which will form the foundation of your sessions. You and your body will profit from this great source of comfort.

Benefits of the Asana of Liberation

Your body already practices this form of breathing subconsciously to help it decompress, relax, and prepare for sleep. The body also emits sighs to preserve itself from nervousness and general fatigue. Your body puts the breath to work automatically but often too late or in an ineffective way. Little by little, your body loses its quality of life.

The Asana of Liberation is intended to increase breathing capacity, purify the blood, oxygenate the muscular fibers, eliminate nervous and muscular tensions and mental fatigue, and awaken the senses. It facilitates the recovery period of both the physical and mental bodies. This asana will give you the means of cooperating with your body and listening to it in order to protect yourself. It will become easier for you to detect uncomfortable, disquieting situations that can diminish your physical or mental capacities in a given moment quickly.

ASANA OF THE SALUTE TO THE SETTING SUN

I have created a flowing yoga, where everything is one long movement governed by the breath. I call it *kung-du-yoga*.

In kung-du-yoga, the Salute to the Setting Sun is an essential and indispensable group of asanas. The purpose of these asanas is to balance and channel the energy within the body in order to improve circulation, increase awareness of your feelings, and promote regular sleep cycles.

Phase 1: The Breathing of the Ocean or the Breath of Awareness

Focus your mental body by concentrating on an external object. This will protect it against any image that disrupts your concentration. It will also provide a safeguard from further images that appear solely from the movement of your breath and the way your body interprets those images, according to the alertness of your senses.

In this asana, inhalation represents the wave that takes form on the horizon before coming to caress the pebbles on the shore. It evokes strength. So, at the beginning of your inhalation, let this strength rise within you like the wave that arrives from afar, growing bigger and bigger in volume as it transports and lifts you to its crest. During this moment when the air whirls around your lungs, let your chest rise like shutters you are opening wide. Following your inhalation, pause to listen to this energy. It will waltz within you and exchange whispers with your welcoming body.

The exhalation is the marvelous moment when these vibrations echo within you, offering you the occasion to feel the changes in your body. This is an important moment, during which you should try to loosen up your body in order to listen to it better and waltz on this ocean of happiness. With each movement of exhalation your body embraces you like a child in love with the present moment when life reveals its full force to you. It embraces and hugs you to tell you how much it loves you. Exhalation is the wave that recedes into the distance and evokes peace.

Throughout your exhalation, tighten the elevator muscles to support the lifting of the diaphragm. Your belly will harden slightly, starting from the outside and working toward the center. At the same time, make sure you progressively relax the muscles in your body. While breathing, you must listen to the song of the sea that awakens within you.

Before starting your asana, guide your body to translate your intentions. Relax the muscles of your face as much as possible, direct your eyes downward and relax them fully. Adopt a neutral expression. Start to breathe deeply and very slowly without forcing the process. Relax your throat fully in order to emulate the breathing of the ocean. You must be sufficiently attentive to feel the heat of your breath caressing your rear nasal passages. After two or three breaths, your physical and mental bodies will respond to this flow and be at your disposal. To practice the Breathing of the Ocean correctly, breathe deeply while keeping the throat relaxed. Pay attention to the amount of breath in the back of the throat and its level. During inhalation, it should be in the upper throat area and for exhalation, in the abdominal region.

It is imperative to hear each distinct movement of your respiration. It should awaken within you images from your body's experience to bring you more easily to your goal of serenity and complete awareness. You will then be supported by the projected image of the ocean, because nearly everyone has seen the movements of the ocean waves that dance and sing with the wind. Your body has stored in its memory this soothing melody within which sweet inner journeys float. Consider your breath to be an immense ocean in motion that regenerates your life, with the movement of the waves awakening your consciousness.

Throughout your asana, be attentive to your body. You must be capable of feeling everything that comes from it. Also, the body must be able to feel everything that comes from you in order to follow you. But don't forget that you are just beginning its education.

Then begin the asana:

• Stand with your legs straight and your arms relaxed at the sides of your body. Turn the palms of your hands toward your body. Make sure your spinal column is aligned correctly from the lumbar (lower back) to the cervical (upper back) vertebrae.

• Keep your heels together and place your big toes at a

Asana of the Salute to the Setting Sun

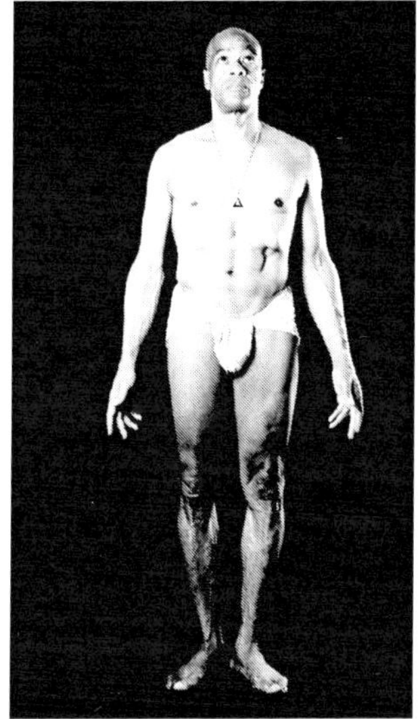

Figure 7

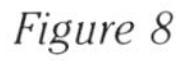

Figure 8

Figure 9

Figure 10

Asana of the Salute to the Setting Sun

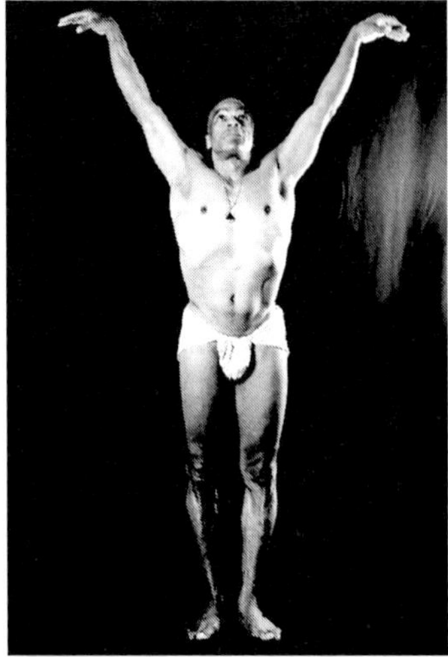

Figure 11

distance of twelve to sixteen inches from one another to form a pyramid between your feet. The point of the pyramid is at the heels (see figure 7).

• Don't forget to separate your feet by about twenty inches.

• As you inhale, raise your arms slowly, straight in front of you. Join your thumbs, relax your wrists, and turn the palms of your hands towards the floor (see figure 8).

• At the end of your inhalation, extend both arms above your head and link the thumbs in a Mudra of the Sun to correct the spinal column's alignment (see figure 9). A *mudra* is a way of positioning the hands and body to seal off the eyes, ears, mouth, etc., keeping the life energy inside the body. It is used during preparation or to close meditation and yoga sessions.

• Once inhalation is completed and your lungs are filled,

raise your face and the palms of your hands toward the sky. Spread your fingers wide and bend them slightly into the shape of claws. Stretch your body along its entire length, right up to your fingertips (see figure 10).

• To exhale, relax your stretch while keeping your arms and spinal column straight. Turn the palms of your hands outward and relax the wrists in order to let your hands fall (see figure 11). At the end of your exhalation, lower your arms in the form of a cross and then downward to the sides of your body.

• During the pause, with lungs emptied, relax your body as much as possible and be attentive to its state. Your asana is completed.

• If your session is limited to the Salute to the Setting Sun, perform a dozen rounds before moving to the next higher stage.

During this asana, the rhythm of your automatic breathing may have a tendency to accelerate, provoking a slight loss of breath. To free your body from tension and rebalance the rhythm of your breathing, perform an Asana of Liberation (see page 55).

The first attempt at this breathing exercise will seem difficult. Give yourself time to learn the Breath of the Ocean. Receive it like the melody of a little breeze caressing your skin. It will awaken delightful sensations within your body and evoke memories of pleasant moments, making you dream of better things.

This breathing exercise will awaken an awareness level that will enable you to rediscover values that all too often escape your notice.

Phase 2: The Breathing of the Yogi

In order to advance and communicate more deeply with your mental body, you must solicit more from it. The mental body is very sensitive; it will not always be present and available to follow you, if you don't know how to maintain it properly.

To do so, try the Breathing of the Yogi. This asana is practically identical to the Breathing of the Ocean. However, the inhalation is centered a little lower in the back of the throat.

The steps in the Breathing of the Yogi are as follows:

- Assume the initial position for the Salute to the Setting Sun, placing your feet correctly in the Mudra of the Pyramid. (see figure 12).
- Lift your arms high while inhaling.
- Lift your heels off the floor. Make them rise and fall simultaneously with your arms, in rhythm with your inhalation.
- Inhalation has three phases:
  1. Inhalation: three seconds
  2. Pause: three seconds
  3. Inhalation: three seconds
- At the end of the last inhalation, stand on your toes to balance your body.
- Turn your face and the palms of your hands to the sky, (see figure 13)
- Following inhalation, pause and stretch for six seconds.
- Before exhaling, take the time to relax your wrists. Turn the palms of your hands to the floor while lowering your arms in the form of a cross, then move them downward to the

Salute to the Setting Sun with the Breathing of the Yogi

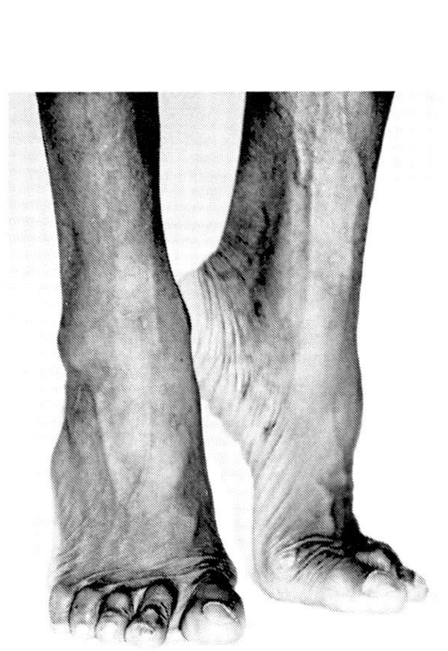

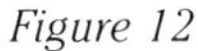

Figure 12

Figure 13

sides of your body during exhalation.

• Exhalation takes place in a single flow. Do it as slowly and deeply as possible while seeking relaxation.

• Finally, there is a six-second pause with lungs empty, which enables you to listen to your body before performing the Asana of Liberation.

• During the six-second pause between breaths, stretch your body fully.

• While still keeping time with your breathing, your heels should slowly descend to the floor.

• After the six seconds' pause with empty lungs, prepare yourself with the Asana of Liberation before starting over again.

Even if the Breathing of the Yogi technique seems fairly difficult, it is completely within your reach. It would be a shame not to offer your body a source of comfort that will improve its life.

There is a way to simplify the Breathing of the Yogi in a "student" version in order to make it more accessible and to facilitate willpower in daily training. I call this the "Breathing of the Young Yogi." Since it is intended to increase your respiratory capacity quickly, it gives you the possibility of building up positive morale to strengthen willpower.

During inhalation, inhale in three stages of two seconds, or six seconds in all, pausing three times for two seconds each also equaling a total of six seconds. This means that you will perform the inhalation in six steps:

1. Inhalation: two seconds
2. Pause of all movement: two seconds
3. Inhalation: two seconds
4. Second pause: two seconds
5. Inhalation: two seconds
6. Third pause: two seconds

In the beginning, your breathing capacity may not be sufficient to perform this asana at its highest level. Don't force yourself, as that would be a form of aggression against your self. Try your best without ever forcing yourself, so that your body does not suffer. To find the correct depth for the breathing movements, you must imagine the breathing of deep sleep (without snoring). Take a long, slow breath that arises from the depths of the throat and is restful to listen to, approximating the song of the ocean's waves. It will require you to pause several times during inhalations so you can focus your concentration better on the balance of your physical body.

Start with the Breathing of the Young Yogi. After about a month of training, your breathing capacity will have increased. You will gradually feel more comfortable in your body. From there, when you think you are ready, and you are taking good care of your body, move on from the Asana of the Student and train with this first variant of the Breathing of the Yogi.

Note how long it took for your respiratory state to improve. You will train for the same amount of time with the new version before returning to the Asana of the Young Yogi. This will allow you to measure the progress you have made.

Additional Points about the Asana of the Salute to the Setting Sun with the Breathing of the Yogi

While raising your arms, make sure you gradually increase the pressure of your buttocks against one another; maintain this pressure until the stretch ends. This posture is extremely effective in helping maintain balance and useful in eliminating painful sciatica from the lumbar region of the back.

During inhalation, when you raise your feet partly, it is imperative to keep the heels touching in order to avoid the risk of a sprained ankle. Be careful: This more difficult asana can be harmful if not performed gradually and with care. Never lose sight of the fact that your body constitutes one of your greatest treasures. Consider yourself the guardian and protector of your body and behave like one.

To reinforce the participation of your mental body and stay balanced on your toes without too much risk or difficulty, focus on a point more than two yards in front of you at ground level. This will serve as your first mental energy point throughout the asana. You also need a second energy point, located directly over the first point. If you are in a room, visualize a vertical line to the ceiling. The second point should be situated in the angle between the wall and the ceiling.

When to Perform this Asana

Although it refreshes the body and can be performed at any time of day, this is a natural evening asana.

Benefits of the Asana of the Salute to the Setting Sun with the Breathing of the Young Yogi

The Breathing of the Yogi will train your physical and mental bodies to focus on images and reinforce their cooperation with your life. By channeling the first movements of energy within your body, you are starting your mental education with a more pronounced awakening of awareness. Soon, you will observe various sensations of hot, cold, and a tingling that moves throughout the body. You have just integrated the initial phase of listening to your body in a search for physical balance. This is based on mental stability, which is the first form of concentration. I call it "external concentration." It promotes the release of stress and improves circulation. It eliminates nervous and muscular tensions. It strengthens the muscles of the lumbar region in order to perfect their alignment and eliminate problems with sciatica. It combats fatigue and strengthens the mind and morale.

As a result of these asanas, you will feel a distinct dilation of the arteries that will provoke a sensation of hot and cold around your body. Your blood is purifying, and the irrigation of the arterial fibers (capillary vessels) is improving. You will also increase your pulmonary capacity. Little by little, smokers will feel repelled by the taste and smoke of cigarettes.

ASANA OF THE YANG WITH THE BREATHING OF THE OCEAN

With your arms at the sides of your body, stand tall so that your spinal column is as straight as possible. Place your feet side by side, flat on the floor, at a distance of two or three inches from one another and with the big toes firmly planted. Spread all the other toes so that they are separate from one another. Take a very deep breath to start pulmonary ventilation. This will help make the blood more fluid. Continue to breathe deeply, relaxing the face and the throat fully to bring your body to a peaceful state. Focus on each of the breathing movements in order to establish coordination between the physical and mental bodies.

Relax your eyes and direct them downward. In order to engage the mental body fully, focus on your energy point at ground level. Draw your breath from it, the energy that will nourish your body. Imagine that you wish to hypnotize this point. This should also help to channel your energy.

The asana is practiced with the help of square breathing: inhale for six seconds; pause with lungs full for six seconds, stretching one side of the body; exhale for six seconds; pause with your lungs empty for six seconds. Take advantage of an exhalation to close your eyes while still keeping your energy point present in your memory. From there,

• Inhale, slowly lifting your left arm in front of you with your wrist relaxed and the palm of your hand turned to the floor.

• Lift your toes and the sole of the left foot from the ground, keeping contact solely with the heel (see figure 14).

• Slide your heel forward. It should never leave the floor or move further forward than the toes of the other foot. Throughout the whole asana, make sure your toes are lifted and spread as much as possible.

• Continue to raise your left arm above your head with your left leg directly in front of you and your heel pressed into the floor (see figure 15).

• With lungs full, turn the palm of your hand to the sky and spread all the fingers from one another, bending them slightly into the form of claws.

• Stretch the left side of your body from your toes to your fingertips while keeping the right side of the body as relaxed

Asana of the Yang with the Breathing of the Ocean

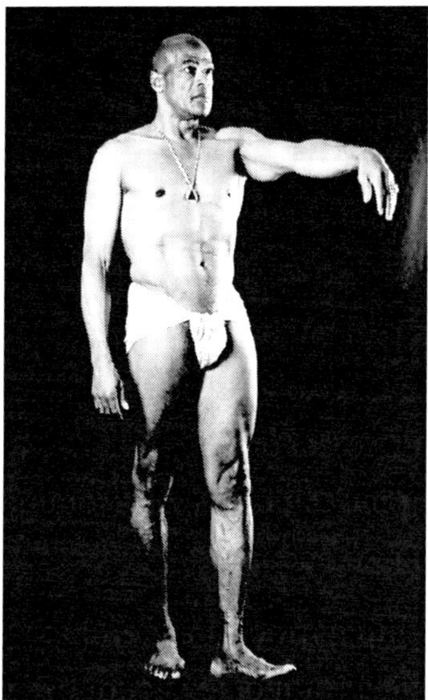

Figure 14

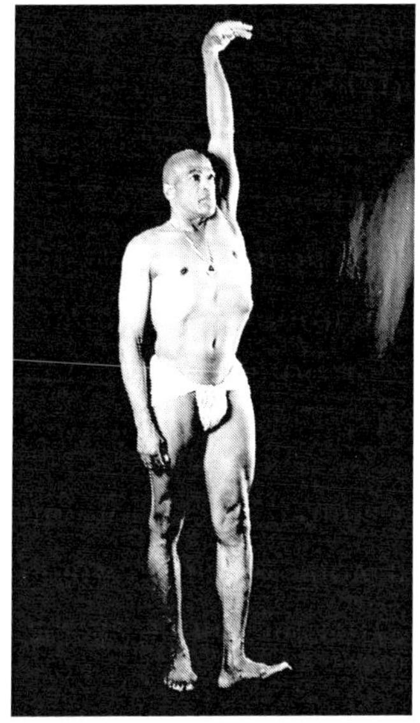

Figure 15

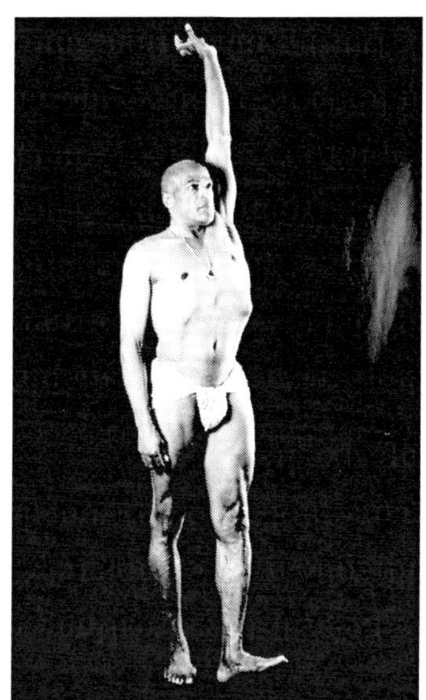

Figure 16

as possible (see figure 16).

• Keep your eyes closed and your face turned to the sky while you stretch throughout the pause in breathing with lungs full.

• To exhale, relax your stretching but maintain the same posture. Keep your eyes closed. Bend your wrist forward and straighten your head. Slowly lower your left arm in front of you, keeping it fully extended.

• Slide your heel backward to return to its starting place.

• When the exhalation is complete and your body returns to its initial position, open your eyes. Keep them open during the pause with lungs empty, in order to find the energy point again.

• Resume your asana. Slowly close your eyes as you begin your next inhalation. This time, work with the right side of your body.

Benefits of the Asana of the Yang

This asana makes the blood more fluid, drains unwanted energy and clears the brain. It eliminates nervous tensions, improves memory, reduces blood pressure, and induces a profound state of peace. However, be careful: You may feel brief sensations of dizziness during your asana, especially during exhalation—the principal phase in which the brain is cleansed. In order to derive the benefits of this asana fully, it is advisable to practice at least five rounds on each side.

ASANA OF THE YIN WITH BREATHING OF THE OCEAN

Stand up with legs straight but supple, your feet separated by about twenty inches. Bend your arms and place your hands upon each other about two inches from your navel. Turn your palms skyward and touch the tips of your thumbs to form a pyramid that will symbolize a Mudra of Energy (see figure 17).

The Asana of the Yin is performed with square breathing of eight: inhale for eight seconds; pause with lungs full for eight seconds; exhale for eight seconds and pause with your lungs empty for eight seconds.

• At the start of inhalation, place your the right hand on your left hand and pivot to turn the fingertips and palm toward the floor.

• Slowly, lift your the right arm to shoulder height (see figure 18).

• With your arm extended before you, turn the palm of your hand towards your face. Bring the arm backwards, keeping it straight (see figure 19).

• Once your arm has reached maximum stretch, flip the wrist backwards, as if you were resting your hand against an imaginary wall.

• Lower your shoulder. Stretch your arm to extend it further. Continue to bring the arm backward so that it can truly reach its maximum extension (see figure 20).

• Fill your lungs with air and hold this posture throughout the pause.

• To exhale, flip your wrist forward to bring the palm of the hand back towards you. Your extended but supple arm should travel downward in the same manner as before.

• Once your arm is in front of you, at shoulder height,

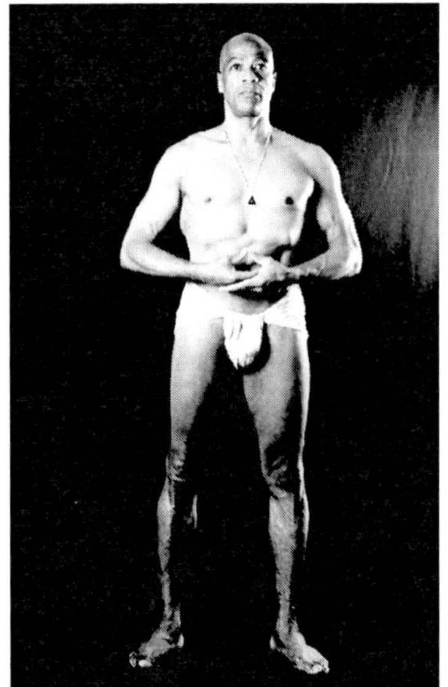

Figure 17

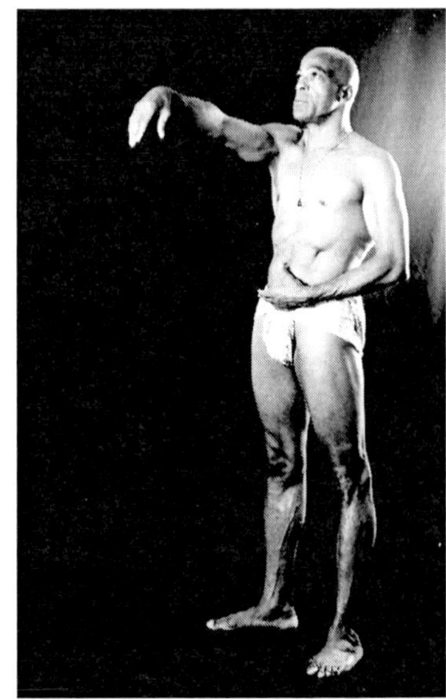

Figure 18

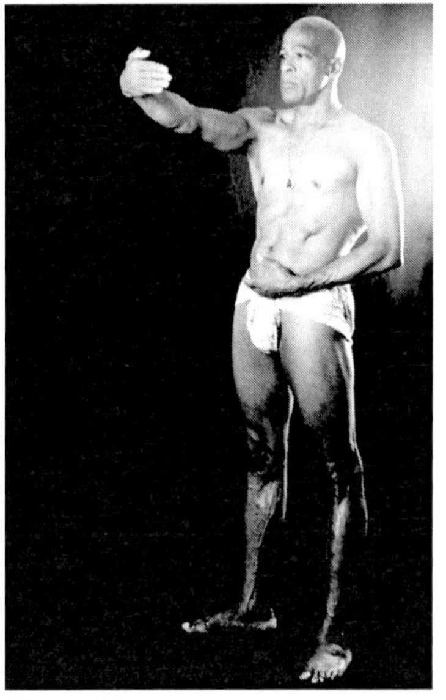

Figure 19

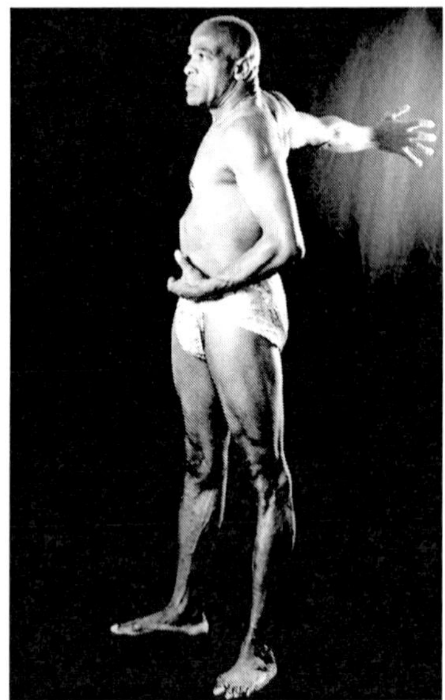

Figure 20

bend it so that your hand moves beneath the other hand.

- Mark a pause, with your lungs empty, before taking up the asana again on the other side.

Benefits of the Asana of the Yin

The Asana of the Yin encourages the cleansing of the brain, which is sometimes liable to cause sudden dizziness. This can be frightening at first, but it's quite normal. Nevertheless, you need to be careful. In the beginning, avoid performing this asana in a place cluttered with low furniture and/or a hard floor, because there is the risk of falling. Always make sure to keep your head straight during the asana while using your eyes to track the path taken by your working arm until it moves beyond your vision.

With practice, your body's functioning will improve greatly, and the sensations of dizziness will disappear. If you do experience dizziness, you can easily suppress it without having to stop your asana. Just close your eyes and clench the eyelids firmly shut for two seconds, then open them. Repeat this two or three times, if necessary. Whatever the reason for your dizzy spells, they will be dissipated.

This asana tones up the eye muscles and the optic nerve, improving vision. It also regulates the body's energy.

KATA OF THE GREAT VENTILATION

A *kata* is a movement or practice that takes you deep within. To perform the Kata of the Great Ventilation:

- Start to inhale from the beginning of your kata, and

Kata of the Great Ventilation

Figure 21

Figure 22

Figure 23

Kata of the Great Ventilation

Figure 24

Figure 25

synchronize your breath with your movements.

• Stretch your right leg fully to the rear. As it arrives behind you, the upper side of the foot will be against the floor, and the sole of your foot turned toward the sky. Your weight will be on your left leg, and the knee will move far forward so that your Achilles tendon is taut.

• Turn the palm of your right hand in the same direction as your face, with you fingers spread and bent slightly in the shape of claws. Lean against an imaginary wall (see figure 21).

• With your lungs full, make sure you form a straight line from the foot to the hand.

• Keep your body stretched out completely during the entire pause in breathing with lungs full.

• From the tips of your toes to the ends of your fingers, your body should be stretched as far as possible (see figure 22).

• Before exhaling, push on your left leg to raise yourself back up.

• Keep your arms in their positions.

• As your body straightens up, let your right foot return naturally to the side of the left foot (see figure 23). You are now standing up straight with your left arm folded in front of you and your right arm extended above your head.

• Stretch your body as much as possible on the right side for about three seconds while trying to inhale a little more. Then begin exhalation.

• At the same time, lower your right hand and make it turn on itself in a corkscrew movement.

• When your right hand reaches the height of your left hand, lower both hands to the sides of your body simultaneously.Your kata is completed.

• Before starting on the other side, separate your feet from one another by twenty inches and perform the Asana of Liberation, which should alternate with each kata.

KATA OF THE GREAT VENTILATION WITH BREATHING OF THE OCEAN

Follow the previous steps, substituting these additional movements where appropriate:

• Stand up, placing your feet at a distance of eight to twelve inches apart.

• Bend your elbows to bring your hands in front of you.

• Point the palm of your right hand toward the sky and point the left palm downward.

• Raise the right foot, keeping only the tip of the toes in

contact with the floor (see figure 24).

• While remaining in contact with the floor, trace an arc with your foot, starting slightly in front of you and moving towards the right and then to the rear (see figure 25).

• At the same time, trace a small arc with your hands in the same direction, crossing one another. Turn the palm of your right hand forward.

• As your left arm come towards the body, extend your right arm forward.

• During this time, let your right foot continue its path.

Benefits of the Kata of the Great Ventilation

The Kata of the Great Ventilation stimulates the memory, improves the automatic coordination of the body, and promotes mental stability and concentration. It also facilitates cleansing the brain, sharpens the physical body's sense of balance, and strengthens the leg muscles.

ASANA OF SLEEP WITH THE BREATHING OF THE OCEAN

This is one of the few asanas that must be performed in three successive phases. It should also be accompanied by two other asanas for the body to derive maximum benefit from it.

Phase 1: Breathing of the Tree Associated with Breathing of the Ocean

• Lie flat on the floor with your legs together and your spinal column as straight as possible. Straighten your arms, turn the palms of your hands toward your body, and make fists (see figure 26).

• Focus your inhalation at the rear of your nose, the movements always taking place at the height of the upper thoracic cage

Breathing of the Tree

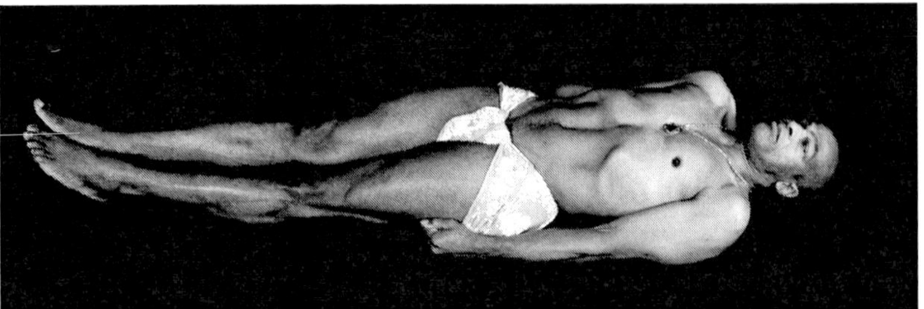

Figure 26

(rib cage containing the heart and lungs). Your inhalation should be particularly invigorating and deep.

• The sound of this inhalation should resemble the dance of branches and leaves of a tree swaying in a violent wind.

• At the same time, and in synchronized fashion, your body should contract like a piece of extremely hard wood.

• Keep this position, with maximum contraction, throughout the pause with full lungs.

• Upon exhaling, slowly and deeply attain the most complete relaxation possible. Start with the scalp and move to the face, throat, shoulders, the thoracic cage, and the belly. Visualize this relaxation as it descends to the soles of your feet. During the pause with empty lungs, watch your body relax.

• The sound of the exhalation, which moves through the rear of the throat, should resemble an ocean wave receding towards the depths after erasing the footprints left on a beach.

• In order to permit yourself to obtain greater coordination between your physical and mental bodies, synchronize your inhalation with the contraction that begins with the belly.

The subsequent relaxation takes place throughout the movement of exhalation, and its pause, when the lungs have been emptied.

• During inhalation, achieve maximum muscular contraction in a minimum of time. During exhalation, concentrate intensely to focus the mental body on relaxing the belly.

Phase 2: The Asana of "Delirious Stretching" with Breathing of the Ocean

Your physical body belongs to this world. God has offered it to you so that you may understand the world as well as to find what lies within you. Fortunately for you, but unfortunately for your body, it is being constantly bombarded with life's messages. Even though you may have neglected your body, it still receives these messages. These messages are aimed at you like arrows, and the number of wounds multiplies daily in the body's flesh. Anxieties and nervous tensions create muscular contractions that make the body a prisoner that is bruised a little more each day by the chains of life down the road to demoralization. Often you don't allow yourself the possibility of accepting these messages in order to understand them.

In order to facilitate your steps toward full comprehension of your body, and to help externalize its feelings, I have created the Asana of Delirious Stretching. It liberates your body, so that it can free itself from nervous and muscular tensions, and your mind can eliminate the preconceptions that reduce its vital space and invoke the impression of being stifled. You will become delirious with your body through a way of seeking that may seem new but in fact has always been available to you.

How many times in your life have you felt a rising sensation of being fed up or of general mental fatigue? This state provokes an irresistible desire to scream or break things, to say no to a whole part of your life—or to leave the present moment and plunge into the unknown for a few hours or days in order to decompress and breathe freely. In reality, these feelings are nothing but cries for help from your body, which has a compelling need to live in health and without hindrance.

Isn't this desire to seek the unknown, to start or start over, simply a distress call from your Higher Self with respect to your being? These influences provoke a permanent conflict between the body that suffers and is forced to pretend, and the being who ignores the fact that it is time. The body does not give itself time to accept. This escalates to the point of leading its body into a state of intolerance and nervousness that destroys it a little more each day. Your Higher Self submits to the influences of the life that surrounds it, along with your body—but when distressed, it issues a call for change.

The unknown is none other than your Higher Self. The unknown exposes the need to encounter your self, to stand alone with whatever is within you that will permit you to understand life and the world, the path that leads to God by way of the Higher Self.

Here are the steps in this asana:

• Lie down on your back with your arms placed alongside your body. Begin the Breathing of the Tree and Breathing of the Ocean.

• While inhaling, raise your arms above your head and link the thumbs to ensure better alignment of the spinal column.

• To achieve this, inhale strongly through the back of the nose, raise the thoracic cage high, and fill your lungs. Don't stop inhaling; keep trying to draw in more air.

• Stretch your body lengthwise, from the top of your head to the ends of your feet.

• After inhaling, raise your toes upward, lifting your head so that you can see them and create an outward extension of the cervical vertebrae (see figure 27). You should feel the effect on the spinal column distinctly. Your breath is still paused, with lungs full.

• Rest your head on the floor, point your toes forward and release your thumbs without worrying about the position of the arms. Tilt your pelvis forward, then back. Turn onto your left side and put your right leg on the floor outside the left leg, with the right leg bent at the knee (see figure 28).

• Your shoulders should remain on the floor. Turn your head to the right as far as you can so that the spinal column is twisted as much as possible, especially in the lumbar region. Don't force it.

• Do the same stretch on the other side. You have just stretched your spinal column in every direction, provoking a call for energy.

• To exhale, halt any movement and relax the body completely. Release air while trying to suppress any

Asana of Delirious Stretching

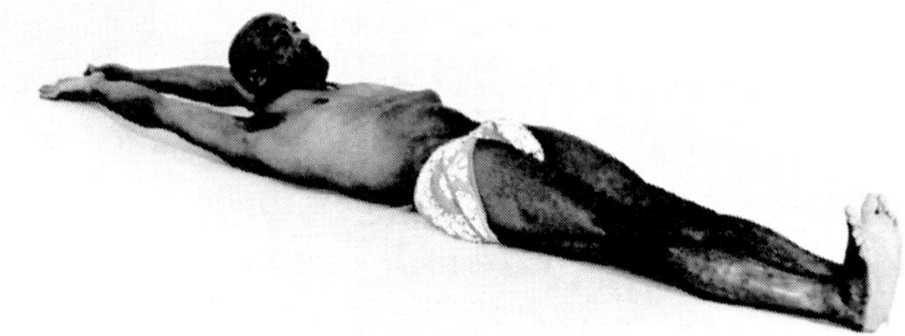

Figure 27

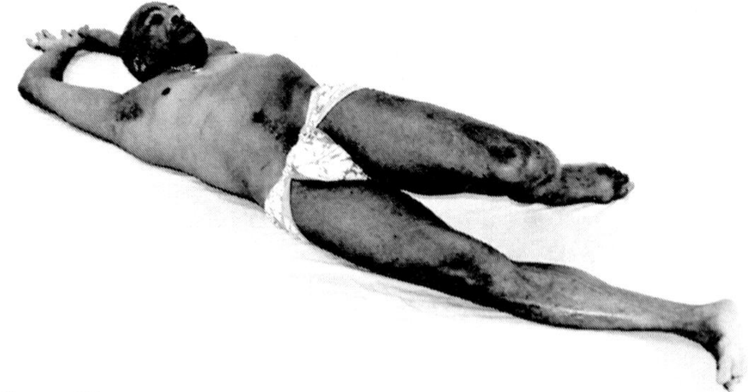

Figure 28

contractions. The asana is completed.

• Remain lying down as you perform the Asana of Liberation two or three times to achieve great ventilation of the lungs, without worrying about the movement of your arms, before starting over.

During the Asana of Delirious Stretching, all movements and times of breathing will be at the limit of your possibilities. Continue to stretch the body as though it were a search for liberation. Detach and deliver your body and being from any tension or blockage. *Become completely delirious* in your stretching efforts.

In the beginning your reduced breathing capacity might be insufficient to carry out this asana. If that's the case, break up your asana into two stages. With training, your respiratory, arterial, and cardiac capacities will improve. Then, it will be possible to perform your asana in a single stage with sufficient ease to improvise the movements at the end so that your body finds complete freedom.

After the asana, you may be a little out of breath, which is by no means abnormal. If your shortness of breath is excessive, then the pause after inhalation was too long for your respiratory capacity. Shorten the pause. You may find that your pulse rate has accelerated too much. This is not a negative development—quite the contrary— but you must let it settle down again before resuming.

Before exhaling, take care to suppress your contractions for one or two seconds, then release the air all at once. After exhalation, mark a pause of two to four seconds, which is useful to remain attentive to your body. Observe and listen to it. Then inhale sharply.

After the movement, continue to take air into the lungs for another four seconds. Relax the throat as much as possible, letting your breath exit like a falling object. Perform this exercise twice. Let your body sigh freely without forcing the breathing movements. I call this the "shy sigh." Normally, your pulse rate should drop by one-half to three-quarters.

This technique works for any situation that causes breathlessness. You can now continue your Asana of Delirious Stretching.

When to Perform this Asana

The Asana of Delirious Stretching can be carried out at any hour. When it is not integrated within a session, it is preferable to repeat it at least a dozen times, so that your body and your morale will benefit completely from it.

The Benefits of the Asana of Delirious Stretching

The Asana of Delirious Stretching eliminates nervous and muscular tensions, balances the body's energy, induces great relaxation and a profound state of peace, and promotes greater sleep. It also helps eliminate backaches and straighten the spinal column into correct alignment, which provides strong relief from pain caused by scoliosis or other spinal deformities.

Phase 3: The Asana of Sleep with Breathing of the Ocean

The purpose of this asana is to complete all of your preceding work. I recommend that you always finish with it. It will provide your mental body with a liberation that will manifest as a state of peace and relaxation. For this reason, yawning will soon play a prominent part. The cooperation between the physical and mental bodies will permit you to drift off in a floating sensation, releasing all tension and demonstrating how your body has found the indispensable harmony it requires to perfect balance.

From the beginning of this asana, prepare yourself to experience a profound and strictly personal moment in which you will take delight with your body. This prayer of love will open the doors of your inner state. You will then be out of reach of any external movement and of all the negative bombardments of the surrounding world. The first element protected will be your mental body, which will boost your morale and build a positive screen for it. In a natural fashion, like water sliding down a mountain slope in search of a plain, the mental body will make sure that your physical body is enveloped in its protective armor.

To practice the asana:

• Lie down on your back with your legs straight, feet together, and arms at your sides.

• Breathe naturally and deeply at least three times. This will assist your physical body to relax better upon each exhalation, so that it understands what you expect of it.

• In addition, isolate yourself from external influences by closing your eyes during exhalation. This introduces light into your inner house so that your mental being, your personal guide, can help you discover your inner space. Without the cooperation of your mental body, your physical body will never achieve the goal being sought.

• With the Breathing of the Ocean, shift your arms slowly above your head in rhythm with your inhalation, and let them trail across the floor (see figures 29–31).

• With your lungs full and arms lying above your head, link your thumbs to support the alignment of your spinal column and stretch your entire body lengthwise (see figure 32). Point your toes as much as you can while still trying to draw air into the lungs.

Asana of Sleep

Figure 29

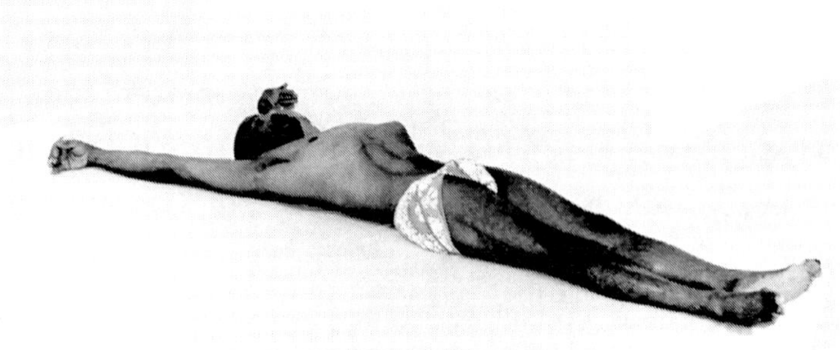

Figure 30

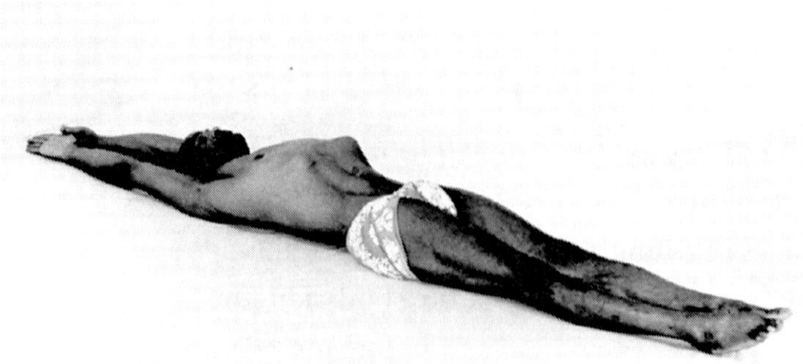

Figure 31

Asana of Sleep

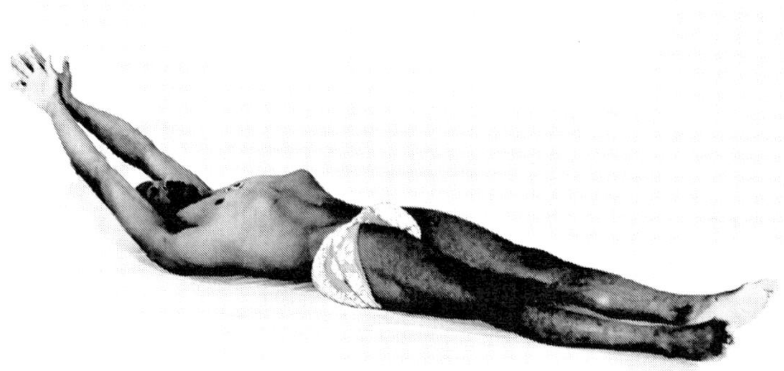

Figure 32

Figure 33

• To exhale, place your hands back to back with your arms well extended. Return them to their initial position by passing over your body (see figure 33).

• At the end of exhalation, suppress any contractions by letting your hands fall on your thighs, then to their starting position on the floor. Pause for two to four seconds with your lungs empty, then repeat.

After four or five Asanas of Sleep, insert a Breathing of Liberation between each asana, before starting over. Help your facial muscles stretch deeply without interrupting your asanas. If the Breathing of Liberation causes you any difficulty, replace it with a deep sigh. Make sure not to stifle your yawns, which will be more and more frequent. On the contrary, try to aid them as much as possible by opening your mouth wide.

In order for your session to be truly profitable, you should perform this asana a dozen times. Between the fourth and fifth rounds, your body will really start to eliminate nervous and muscular tensions—one of the reasons for yawning. Don't put your hand over your mouth (an almost automatic movement to shield the inside of the mouth from the sight of others), because this gesture will awaken blockages that risk hindering the goal being sought here. Similarly, it is futile to try to wipe tears from your eyes. Try to ensure that your focus remains solely on your seeking, because each of your asanas must be better than the preceding one, and the satisfaction of your body must grow deeper.

After completing this series, keep your initial position for about five minutes. Try not to move your limbs, not even an inch. Relax your body as much as possible, keeping the eyes closed. Don't worry any longer about your breathing. Let your body live automatically and respond spontaneously, and content yourself with simply being. Be attentive, docile, and in love with this body which is waiting to give to you.

This is a manner of listening and of telling it that you are with it, that you live with it, and that you are at ease with it. Even if this encounter is disturbed by yawning, whose unfurling you must always allow, keep in mind that you are in the most important phase of your seeking, the instant in which you must create the link. So apply yourself!

When you start listening, you will be disturbed by repeated yawns and coldness in the feet and hands. You might even shiver. These reactions signify that you have lowered your blood pressure by eliminating nervous and muscular tensions. Consequently, your body temperature has dropped in order to find its balance better. When this happens, bring your session to a close and dress warmly, or else slide comfortably into bed to regenerate yourself with a sleep that will be much deeper than you have known previously.

After several days of practice, you may be carried off to sleep during the session without realizing it. At first glance, you may take this as a favorable sign; I can't permit myself to contradict you. However, if sleep carries you off without you being aware of preventing it through simply modifying your breathing, your body was in need of it. These few seconds of sleep will be equivalent to hours of normal recuperation.

Nonetheless, it is preferable to remain awake in order not to lose contact with this body that has just sent you a distress signal by falling asleep. Indeed, each time you sleep, the seeking of the deep link between you and your body will be interrupted. This supplementary step toward your supreme fulfillment will have to wait until another day. During sleep, the body is left to its automatic responses. The muscles that seem relaxed are actually contracting slowly, and agitation caused by small brusque movements is possible.

In this first phase of sudden sleep, your subconscious will search the body's memory for images of its experience in order to translate them. You will enter a phase of deep dreaming. Through this sleeping state, you have just lost a precious moment of life, because the seeking of the body-mind link is considered to be a prayer of love and of gratitude. Breath becomes a caress that leads to the birth of the senses. Through its complex functioning and infinite number of interpretations of its reactions, the body becomes the infinite insofar as it serves as the indispensable vehicle for our supreme fulfillment and uplifting.

Has something really been lost? Not really, because until the body finds peace and serenity, nothing is possible.

When to Perform This Asana

The Asana of Sleep prepares the body for sleep. I strongly advise that you perform this asana at the end of the afternoon or in the evening, just before going to bed.

The Benefits of the Asana of Sleep

The Asana of Sleep is highly recommended for combating fatigue, stress, and mental agitation, as well as any form of nervousness or problems with insomnia. It will also balance energy and improve the body's irrigation. As a result, it regenerates morale and makes it highly positive.

ASANA OF CATALEPSY

Catalepsy is an attack of fitfulness. This asana will help prevent it.

The Asana of Catalepsy is performed with trapezoidal Tree-Ocean Breathing: Inhale for three seconds; pause with your lungs full for six seconds; exhale for six seconds; and pause with your lungs empty for six seconds.

Perform this asana a dozen times. In the beginning, you may feel pain in certain parts of the body, or a cramp might develop against your will, most frequently in the foot or calf muscles. This is quite normal. Don't let it stop your asana. These unpleasant little moments will disappear with practice. Very quickly, your body will derive a great benefit and sense of ease from the hygienic movements you have begun to adopt. Your muscles will no longer be asphyxiated, your blood will be cleaner, and your body will gain living comfort.

THE ASANA OF THE CATALEPSY OF THE MASTER, OR RELAXATION

It is so pleasant to exist within a body that lives serenely and accepts external influences, without submitting to them but regarding them as messages to perfect understanding. The body uses this knowledge to protect itself from systematic contractions caused by the thousands of spontaneous reactions it experiences every day. These contractions induce physical fatigue and affect morale. As they increase in strength, they generate a persistent lassitude.

Learning to relax in any circumstance is a way of guiding your body on the path of fulfillment and a way of teaching it to breathe better. Relaxation enables you to observe the body better in order to understand its necessity in your life. Without relaxation, your body will be like an abandoned child in a hostile, heartless world. Give your body what you expect from life—the time to understand it in order to appreciate and accept it. Give your body the love, respect, and passion that arouses faith. If you take this path, love will be born within you like the morning sun that gives birth to the rainbow adorning the countryside, from which you take such pleasure in beholding. You will meet yourself.

A body that maintains its relaxation is like a child who smiles at the happiness inscribed in the eyes of the person gazing at him. Breathe relaxation like one bestows a kiss, when the heart's loudspeaker awakens the echoes of love and lets its generosity be exhaled. All seeking depends on the understanding and controlling of the breath, or pranayama. It will forever remain the first link in the chain of your life. Breathing will give your body the signal that it can confide in you.

During every one of your breathing exercises, make sure that your mental being tries to gaze and listen through each of the movements of respiration, because it is breath that allows you to discover the inner space of your house. Lie down on your back with legs and arms extended, the palms of your hands turned towards your body and your feet touching each other. Breathe normally but deeply. After two or three breaths, make use of an exhalation to relax the muscles of your face, closing your eyes to help your mental being isolate itself from external influences. Continue to breathe deeply and sufficiently to focus the mental body on the feet. Imagine that you see your feet; it's essential that you feel them.

Guide your body so that one day you will succeed in your encounter, the meeting with the higher self that opens the path to illumination. For that to happen, consider your physical body to be a child you hold by the hand to steady its slow, delicate steps on the staircase leading to the higher self. In this seeking, you will need the physical body, the vehicle you learn to understand in order to travel better; and the mental body, the intimate light that shows you the way to your path.

Each of these two bodies makes use of the projection of an image. When your body is awake, you call this "imagination." In reality, this projection is a guardian, a curator of already-lived experience—the memory of your physical body. It will awaken different sensations so that consciousness will expose them to you and suggest to the mental body that it seek the source of these sensations. In turn, the mental body will search among the physical body's already-lived experiences in order to recover colors and forms that the eyes may have seen previously, the sounds and noises the ears may have heard, the odors and sweet fragrances the nostrils may have inhaled, the touches that may have been received, and the caresses that the hands and the body may have interpreted.

You can assist your own process by creating helpful images. Imagine breath to be a round form stuck beneath the soles of your feet. To do this, perform the Breathing of the Ocean. With each inhalation, feel energy running through your body from the feet to the head, as though covered by a sheet. As it rises, the round form of the energy rolls itself up in the sheet to reveal your body from feet to head. At the end of your inhalation, keep your breath suspended with lungs full for about two seconds, which will give you time to observe. Exhale and send the breath on a downward descent that covers the body with the sheet down to the soles of the feet. During the four seconds when you pause with your lungs empty, keep your mental being focused on the soles of your feet. Try to relax them as much as possible.

Continue the Breathing of the Ocean, along with seeking to focus mentally on the physical body, for five to ten minutes. Control your breath fully and listen constantly to your body, giving it the comfort and pleasure of being free with you. Always give yourself time to listen to your breath so that the melody of each respiration creates a rhythm of the life that belongs to you and which your body must learn to appreciate. Happiness is found in the breath that makes a body sing with love.

When you start out, you will have to listen to your breath distinctly, because the song of breathing enables the mental being to activate the images of your body's memory. This is one way of awakening that marvelous moment when you were the witness of the waves being born in the ocean, flirting with the setting sun. That day, perhaps without even knowing it, your body interpreted this emerging beauty of your senses and movements of energy born from scenic splendor. The body is necessary to appreciate life and to give meaning to your life. Don't forget that your body needs a caress when you gaze at it.

You have taken the time to prepare both your physical and mental beings, to let them know that you need their cooperation so that they understand what you expect of them. This also gives you the opportunity to discover their influence on one another. With peace and serenity, you will possess the means of permitting the body to attain relaxation.

THE CATALEPSY OF THE MASTER

How does someone who has not learned to understand relaxation attain it? To answer this question, I will show you the path.

• Lie on your back, arms at the sides of your body, and perform the Breathing of the Ocean. Close your eyes so you can to gaze inside yourself better.

• Practice the Breathing of the Yogi deeply. After the third breath, your inhalations will be interrupted so that you may observe better. Your mental being remains focused on your feet in order to find and look at energy.

• Inhale for two seconds. Straighten your feet as much as possible, stretching the Achilles' tendons by bending the toes in order to extend the contractions to the knees. The following two seconds' pause will channel your contraction from the foot to the knee and keep it there.

• Resume inhaling for another two seconds.

• In a synchronized fashion, continue the contraction from the knee to the hip. Clench your fists. Then, use the two seconds' pause to channel your contraction again, this time from the foot to the hip.

• Resume inhaling for two more seconds, while continuing to advance the contraction to the top of the head. Clench your jaw tightly, with lips shut and contracted in the form of sending a kiss.

• Finally, at the peak of your inhalation, keep your lungs full for six seconds in order to visualize the totality of your body and heighten your contraction.

• Slowly and calmly, start to exhale. As gently as this breath that caresses your body, let your relaxation descend to the soles of your feet. Let your slow, deep exhalation be carried out in a single continuous flow.

• At the end of this exhalation, keep your lungs empty for six seconds in order to listen to the body and follow its growing relaxation.

• Resume your inhalation for the two seconds that serve to contract the body from the feet to the knees.

• After pausing for two seconds, deepen your contraction from the knees to the hips. Don't forget that you must ignore any cramps in your feet and knees.

• Resume your inhalation and the contraction from the hips to the top of your head. As you pause for six seconds with your lungs full, try to ensure that your physical body makes the contraction as total as possible.

You have just entered the preparation for the most important phase in your seeking. Once you start to exhale, your mental body will give birth to the sensations, awakening images—the key to surrender and escape in your relaxation. Little by little, you will feel the moment come when your conscious being and your body will start to fuse. During the ten minutes or so that you perform this relaxation, your mental body should remain constantly focused on the synchronization of the physical body's inhalation and contractions.

Always consider each of your sessions a privileged moment of dialogue with your body in seeking the harmony that leads to unity.

The Benefits of the Catalepsy of the Master or Relaxation

The mental body regenerates itself in order to rejuvenate the physical body better. The face recovers the serenity and the smile that flirts with happiness. The physical body recuperates its tone and luminosity.

ASANA OF THE PATH OF MEETING (RELAXATION)

Allow your body freedom from its anxieties, so that you can meet it face-to-face without constraints. Let yourself float and navigate in your inner space, in search of what you are and to meet the body as it is. Do this by approaching it in a manner that demands the greatest consideration and determination in your decision to free your body and meet your Higher Self.

Lie down on your back, with your spinal column, legs, and arms all kept straight (see figure 34). Your hands should be about twelve inches from your sides, with your palms turned toward the sky. The distance between your feet should be

Asana of the Path of Meeting

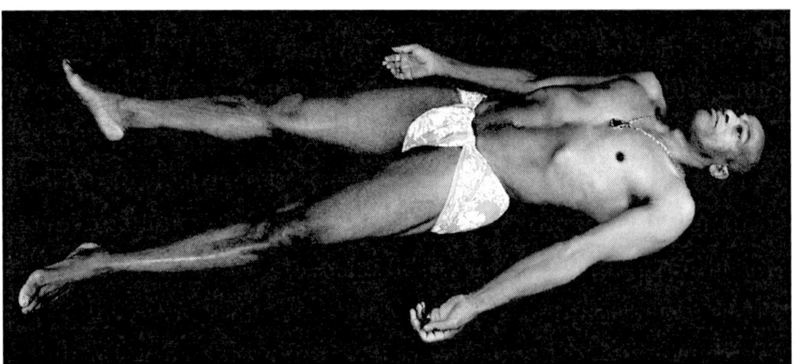

Figure 34

about twelve to fifteen inches. Make sure your body is thoroughly relaxed. Your knees and feet should turn outward in a natural fashion.

To facilitate the straightening and relaxation of the spinal column, lift the buttocks and tilt the pelvis backward in order to press the lumbar vertebrae into the floor; try to avoid any muscular contractions. Even if your protesting lumbar vertebrae try to return to their spontaneous, if sometimes damaging, position, don't worry about them.

The cervical vertebrae also require your attention. They, too, have a tendency to lift from the floor. To straighten them, draw in your chin between your shoulders without lifting your head.

Your cervical and lumbar vertebrae support more of the weight of your daily efforts than you might believe, and they tire easily. Little by little, they lose their alignment and harbor rheumatic troubles that give rise to stabbing pains.

Take advantage of this deep muscular release to reinforce the cohesiveness between the physical and mental bodies. Constantly associate the movements of your breath with gazing upon these two bodies.

• Resume by performing the Breathing of the Ocean. Try to make each of the movements of your breathing deep without exaggeration. Pause for six seconds after each movement.

• After two or three breaths, make use of an exhalation to relax the muscles of the face while closing your eyes. This will foster the isolation that will protect you from external influences so you can concentrate on your seeking.

• Focus your mental being on the soles of the feet, as if breath were drawing its source from this point of the body. Consider breath as a caress, a sheet of sweetness as light as the down of a baby bird that barely brushes your body.

• During inhalation, gaze at this sheet rolling itself up from the feet to the head, like a caress rising up your body to awaken your senses.

• When inhalation is complete, make sure to relax the scalp and face in order to find the gentleness and the child's look of goodness that sleeps within you and smiles at life.

• During this six-second pause with lungs full, keep the mental body focused upon this image of the child's face that transmits love.

• Gently start your exhalation and relax from the head to the toes. Watch the sheet slowly unroll, inviting you to enter the depths of a caress that frees your body of its tensions in order to teach you to discover its sensations.

This exercise will permit you to enter into profound communication with your physical and mental bodies. You will be submerged in images and sensations that you must accept as a docile and accommodating spectator, but without submitting to them. After a while, stop trying to control your breathing, but let it settle naturally like a gentle wave that caresses the shore. Allow your body to experience the sensations that have been awakened with sweetness and fulfillment. Your breathing is automatic; listen to it awaken within your body the life that provokes its transformation. Like a boat floating on the ocean, watch your body follow the bobbing of the waves that bear and transport it far from the movement of the life that surrounds it, to the state of its life that you breathe and contemplate in order to find your self.

Dedicate each of the movements of inhalation to the discovery of your body. Watch it intensely to rediscover your own existence. During the pause when your lungs are full, you must look at it intently and passionately, and it will embrace you.

When the moment of exhalation arrives, relax your body so it becomes fluid like the breath of life that carries it and transports you to an inner personal space. Within this inner space, you will see images inviting you to dance like children who smile at love. You will see your body take form in order to transform itself better and call upon its senses. Gaze upon it in order to listen to yourself better, and you will discover new meaning in your life.

When to Perform this Asana

Perform this practice session as often as you can, for as long as you desire. Each time, choose a moment when you can isolate yourself and take the time to prepare for your session physically and mentally.

Benefits of the Asana of the Path of Meeting

After several days of practice, beauty will emanate from your body, and your face will be so luminous and sparkling that it will transmit the sun to the hearts of all those who come near you.

If you don't understand the language of thought, you can easily stumble down the path of the seven torments—the seven reincarnations, according to the sacred texts. You will walk seven times through the labyrinth of your seven lives without ever finding the exit, much less yourself. This infernal precipice induces the intoxicating euphoria of repetition and the perpetual resumption of a misunderstood life.

In order not to confuse "wanting" and "thinking you want," seek the purpose that has given birth to the image of each thought. In this purpose, you will find your goal without ever forgetting to ask yourself the question, "why." You will find the path, the "how" that will open the door of meditation for you and strengthen the purpose of your goal. In this manner, willpower will be born within you.

However, when the "why" evolves into the question, "How will I go about attaining my goal?" don't rush off like a wild horse that becomes intoxicated with the sound of his hooves and takes leave of his senses. Sit down and seek within you the Buddha (the guide) who will enlighten you with wisdom in order to lead your body with tranquility upon the path. Give your body the time that has been given you, in order to share serenity with it. You will appreciate listening to it and gazing at it in order to watch yourself grow. You will understand that life has always been both simple and marvelous.

Rare are the children of God who take the trouble to look at life as an infinite and luminous richness, and who do not content themselves with merely seeing and submitting to it. One must breathe life as if caressing it in order to better exist within it.

In life, evil does not exist. But man takes pleasure in doing harm to himself for reasons that are not evil, at first glance. Conduct yourself like a child of the Buddha's spring. Don't expect a path strewn with petals and embalmed with perfume of the lotus blossom to soften your steps and caress your nostrils. Walk towards your goal by keeping in mind the image of acceptance, because you are in this world in order to accept it. Whatever difficulties there may be, whatever obstacles you may encounter, don't let them erase your purpose. On the contrary, make use of them to develop the obstinacy that will nourish your strength.

Never think that being stubborn is a fault for one who knows what he wants. In order to facilitate the images of your meditation and make the wisdom of Buddha grow within you, accept that a fault can be just a badly managed virtue.

Whatever is done, thought, or said concerning you, never

let it worry you. Accept everything without passing judgment. However, watch closely for those who put obstacles in your path with the firm intention of harming you. Their reasons will comprise the mirror that will show you the image of what you were yesterday and will no longer be tomorrow.

Remember: There are no real problems. Man makes his life a problem.

Gaze with your breath so that the images of feelings that call forth emotion are born within your body. Gaze at the splendors of life, those you can never find through the images transmitted by the eyes. The subtlety of life bears with it the glow of its beauty and simplicity.

If you content yourself with merely seeing rather than learning to gaze, life will seem so complicated that you will be like a leaf carried off by the whirlwind. You will never be able to choose your own resting place, but will be obliged to settle wherever the wind takes you.

And that is not life, just misery.

Find the happiness of living in the fullest existence, to give to your body what it has always been asking from you, without your having understood: your gaze. Breathe with the spirit of the fresh countryside air in the first glimmerings of morning, caressing your nostrils, enriching your lungs, awakening your life.

I want to give you the key of love's breath that one day will be found in your gaze. With this breath, caress your body as if you were breathing a flower that offers its soul through its fragrance. Receive the strength that you have lacked until now, so that one day you can become a sun. I want you to build your wanting so that you never confuse it with thought, although it is thought that gives birth to such desire.

It will not be enough simply to do what I say in order to succeed. You must search within yourself for the desire that will enable you to make the decisions leading to your goal. Although I am the switch for you, I will never be your light.

The light is within you. Take care of yourself.

CHAPTER 4

Mastery and Self-Control

The word "mastery" implies vanity when used to invoke one's self-proclaimed spiritual wizardry over the body, mind, and world. It also conveys that a struggle has taken place between you, your physical body, and their inner conflicts from which you have emerged victorious.

In the context of this book, we are exploring a different definition of "mastery" than what you're used to following in your lives, since mastery is almost always associated with "dominion over" something, someone, or some teaching. In this case, we're talking about the physical body's natural, instinctual mastery over you—the cause of countless problems in life due to our naturally reactive states.

We are exploring how mastery pertains to the physical body, its relationship to the body's automatic reflexes and spontaneous reactions, and how the higher mental body can control the process to create a higher, more enduring mastery. This is essential for expressing life to the fullest and for using the breath as the guiding force in your life. For example, seasoned long-distance runners will finish their races with an intentional "kick"—a surge of energy that gives them a quicker time or enables them to pass opponents. That "kick" is a spontaneous reflex to finish the race. Even a beginning runner who has conserved energy can experience the natural physical mastery of the body as it takes over, but only if the body has energy left. However, experienced runners will spend months or years finishing their training runs with "kicks" to condition the body's muscles to automatically respond when they are exhausted at race time. This is true mastery, combining an instinctual act of the physical body—the need to finish the race—with mental preparation and concentration to effect the desired result—a strategically timed burst at the end.

This leads to the real truth of mastery: "control," that is the master word. You owe it to yourself to accept the task of controlling the body and teaching it how to live better.

The first step in this process is to note the awakening of mastery that brings about a change in the state and functioning of the body. This enables you to become aware of the tendency everyone has to follow the body's reactions unconsciously. Only after making this observation can you listen to your body and learn how it functions. Instead of allowing your body to react spontaneously—to "kick" too soon in a race or fall out of a yoga posture too soon, for example—you will be able to act effectively. If you merely accompany the body's spontaneous reactions, you will create imbalances and nervous tension.

Without the mind to provide control and concentration, physical mastery is mechanical. Its role is defensive. It aids the body's ability to adapt to changes. A protective guardian, it sets up a state of self-defense. But through lack of knowledge, you can make an enemy out of the body that its natural mastery is supposed to protect.

At the very first hint of change within the body, the level of consciousness, a mental body attribute, reveals anomalies in the physical body which can be overwhelming. Consciousness leads us to observe an evolution in the body's functioning. The mental body will amplify the irregularities and accelerate their negative aspects so they can no longer be stopped.

Because this body isn't you, it is your life. It reveals to you the life that you have been given, that surrounds you and upon which your body depends. Every day, it will tell you, "I need you to live better, just as you need me to exist."

You can consider mastery as a medicine but never as the remedy. In the short term, it provides momentary relief, but this only allows it to wreak further destruction in the future, in a much deeper way. Forget about physical mastery as a goal. Try to look closely at it without encouraging it. Let it be your guide. It will teach you how your body functions. It is up to you to be sufficiently available and attentive to understand mastery in order to control it, to guide the process for the sake of its life.

Bear in mind that your body does not need to be mastered by you. That would be treating it like a slave. Don't ever seek to impose life upon it—it *is* life. On the other hand, you must learn from it. That way, you will understand that the body represents all forms of life. It is the mirror that reflects everything that lives.

If you learn to listen to your body, to respect it, and love it, you will see how beautiful it is to look at others and give them what is growing within you—compassion. This opens the door to a love *that leads to consideration* before returning to love. You will see the positive in situations that might appear to be totally negative. Your body will give you signals that point to the understanding of all things. You will transform these negative signposts into positive messages.

Consider the pains of the body to be such messages. They will come to you like a child who calls out to you at a moment when you're busy with something else, or like a loved one who tells you that the messages of your love are not sufficiently luminous, even though you love him or her with all your being.

Your body is unique and constitutes a whole system. It is the sole portal through which everything passes and leads you to the unity of life. Learn to close your eyes without moving, hugging your own body against you, and enveloping it with your breath of love like a benediction that you pass to the universe in its entirety.

YOU DON'T HAVE A STOMACHACHE; IT'S YOUR STOMACH THAT HAS THE ACHE

Here is an example you can verify in everyday life. You're absorbed by a precise and exacting task that demands significant mental concentration to execute the task being undertaken perfectly. Your belly has been aching for a while (but note that you don't have a stomachache; it's only a part of the body belonging to you that aches). Due to your level of concentration, your mental body (the envelope of the intellect and consciousness) keeps the door to your conscious thinking mind wide open. The task consumes maximum energy, so that all the other levels in your body lay dormant. That explains how you are able to ignore the pain, although it has lasted for several long minutes.

At some point, content with your work, you will breathe deeply while stretching. Your body will interpret this as a moment of release, relaxation, and satisfaction, and will momentarily cause the mind to rest. At the same instant as you exhale (the sigh of a well-deserved rest) in enjoyment, your consciousness will understand it can wake up to report the state of your body to you—you have a pain in your stomach. But since you think the body is you, and you are the body, you will interpret this as, "I have a stomachache."

This is a serious mistake. This statement makes it very difficult to dissociate the pain of the body from the pain of the being. Your mind will amplify the ache in order to transmit it to the mental body, which will provide it with the necessary energy to develop the symptoms. Your pain will become more and more present because, like you, the mental body confuses itself with the physical, and the two bodies are often in conflict. The mental body takes almost complete charge of the ache, which will then grow until it becomes unbearable.

At this point, if you try to resume work, it will be difficult or even impossible. The attention you give to the pain is now three times greater than before, even though the pain isn't three times greater.

The use of the intellectual, thinking level isn't as clear as before, because you are lacking in concentration. From time to time, without even being aware of it, you place a hand on your stomach, as if this spontaneous and unconscious gesture will send magnetic vibrations to suppress your suffering.

With greater insistence, your mental body asks your consciousness to inform it of the state of your body. Now you observe that this ache, which was almost imperceptible at the start, has become unbearable. Before your consciousness awakened, the pains only belonged to your physical body. Now, your mental body is taking on something that wasn't intended for it. Your physical body is not only defending itself against pain but also against its own mental body.

Like all other bodies, the physical body has fifteen different levels—including a mental level that tries to think in the body's place and triggers an automatic self-defense mechanism. Your breathing changes and adopts rhythms that provoke contractions in the painful area. Nervous tensions increase, and circulation is hampered. Provoked by the pain and fed by ignorance, you notice yourself becoming irritated because of the disturbance you feel in your work and your helplessness. You must learn to better understand the body's masterful ability to announce its imbalances.

To understand the body better and help it in any situation, base your response on breathing, which is the very essence of life. Breathing modifies itself according to such circumstances as pain. Be attentive to the movements of breathing. It is one of the best paths for learning to gaze at your body, to understand and help it. By training yourself to help your body today, you clear the path so that tomorrow it can give you the opportunity and means of finding your Higher Self.

Here's an example to put into practice. If you have an ache in your stomach, it's due to an irregularity in the body. Since consciousness shepherds the body's correct functioning, it will carry out its protective task as soon as possible. In addition to the ache, there will be changes in your breathing. In order to relieve the ache, your body will transform your breathing naturally and automatically. Your lung capacity will be reduced to move the belly as little as possible during both inhalation and exhalation, provoking a progressive contraction across this part of your body. Your body has entered a state of self-defense. You have observed the change without seeking to understand the reason; you've sustained it by trying to contract your stomach in a way that hinders correct breathing. You say to yourself, "This is fantastic. I've mastered the pain!"

However, without knowing it, you have committed an aggression against your body and become its enemy. You are hindering your breathing, poisoning your blood, and reducing the level of oxygen in your body. This is called mastery. It is always exercised at the expense of the physical body.

For someone who does not know how to understand, listen to, and control his body, it's dangerous to seek this mastery. The body will defend itself against both the pain and the action taken to suppress it. Your action upsets the self-defenses that the body has naturally put into place. The worst thing is that you have awakened other pains that threaten to take hold for quite a while—like a buzzing in the ears that is likely to last many days or many nights in an extremely tiresome way.

There's a simple test to verify this. If you lean over right now to pick up an object lying on the ground, you will feel your head grow heavy, perhaps in a painful way. Your blood pressure will pound through your ears in time with your heartbeat. Parts of your body may even begin to contract nervously, independent of your will.

A few days later, this unpleasant moment will have been erased from your memory. Yet your body will keep the trace. You will feel weary and tired, for no apparent reason.

How do you help your body protect itself? The best way is to look after your breathing, this fine pearl of life and wonder of nature. All the riches of the world are found in breath. It gives birth to the inspiration that awakens all sensation, all states of being, and all forms of strength.

The light leading to knowledge is the breath that causes your body to live. You must never lose sight of this notion. Treat your body like a child that you breathe into to better love, gaze upon to better understand, and listen to in order to better protect.

This body is the means that God has given you to obtain your goals. Your stomach aches because the solar plexus has accumulated tension. The reason could simply be an unhealthy diet that has provoked a slight poisoning, which would explain the stomach's defensive state. It could be the result of a reckless transition from cold air to warm. Or, the upset could have arisen from your own constitution: Once a month, for two to four days, the body is transformed and is prone to discomforts, of which stomachaches are a part.

Before rushing to your medicine cabinet, try to understand the reason for your stomachache. You may be stressed from accumulating various aggressions without being able to help the body eliminate its nervous and muscular tensions. This seems as impossible as erasing the images of stray negative thoughts from your mind. They constantly create the turbulence of unanswered questions deep within you, to the point where you feel trapped in a long tunnel through which you walk without hope of finding the exit.

Whatever the reason, breathing will permit you to rid yourself of this trouble and offer the body a ray of sunshine that infuses its life. Since everything in your body depends on breathing, your thought must go to this. Breathing will lead you to an awakened body.

ASANA OF THE BENEFICENT OCEAN

This asana will help you understand why breathing can be considered an ocean of life's movements.

Seek refuge in a calm place to seclude yourself from external influences. Close your eyes. Stand up, with your spinal column as straight as possible. Move your arms behind you with your fingers entwined on your buttocks or in contact with the lumbar vertebrae (lower back) to facilitate the tilting of your pelvis.

Breathe slowly and very deeply to focus your mind on your physical body and achieve more rhythmic breathing. Keep your eyes closed as you perform several breaths, prolonging each exhalation. Contract your abdominal wall slowly but forcefully in rhythm with your breath. Once you have completed an exhalation, maintain the ventral (abdominal) contraction for six seconds with lungs empty before repeating your breath (see figure 35). In order to obtain the indispensable cooperation between your mental and physical bodies, visualize your breath enveloping your entire body like two large hands filled with love. Try to feel the air penetrate your body and exhale through your nostrils.

Asana of the Beneficent Ocean

Figure 35

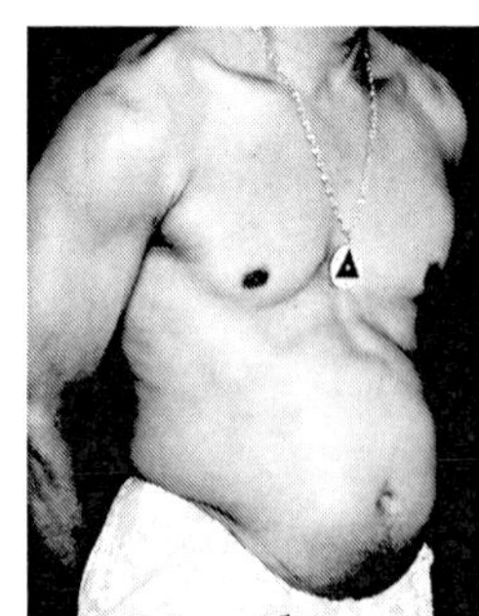

Figure 36

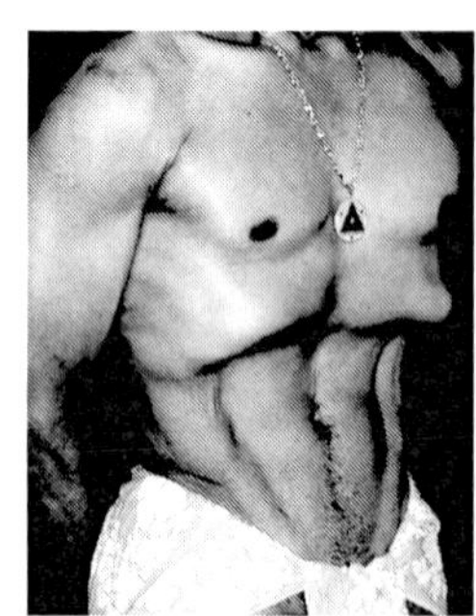

Figure 37

When you think you have achieved the necessary concentration and control, then you can start the Asana of the Beneficent Ocean:

• As the air enters your lungs, push your belly out as far as you can, filling it with the air you inhale.

• To facilitate the movement and invigorate your lumbar vertebrae, raise your hands to this region of your back (opposite the navel).

• As you inhale, tilt your pelvis forward (see figure 36).

• When your inhalation is complete, continue to push your belly out for about three seconds with your lungs filled.

• Exhale by releasing the air very gently, in rhythm with the whole movement.

• At the same time, lower your hands to your buttocks in order to tilt the pelvis backward slightly. Pull in your belly and seek to hollow it as much as possible (see figure 37).

• While keeping the lungs empty, repeat the abdominal movements three times. Let the belly expand as far as possible for one second, then pull it in completely for one second.

• After three such movements with empty lungs, resume your inhalation.

The average breathing times for the asana are six seconds for inhalation, three seconds for a pause with lungs full, six seconds for exhalation, and six seconds for a pause with lungs empty. The minimum recommended length of the session is five to seven minutes.

The Asana of the Beneficent Ocean can be performed standing, sitting, or lying down. After performing the asana, you will feel the need to stretch your body or yawn. As mentioned earlier in the book, don't refrain from doing this, because your body will interpret the stretches as caresses and the yawns as kisses. Your body reflects a great part of what you are. To be at ease, it needs to feel tenderness through the love that comes from you, so that this love can emanate freely and spread throughout its life.

In this asana, you have created a communications link between your physical and mental bodies, through the warmth of the movements of breath. I use the word "warmth" to help you understand that you must consider all these exercises as expressions of endearment, deeply tender gazes you lavish on your physical body that bears witness to your existence. Your body will feel your consideration and will immediately transform your attentions into a dialogue of love and understanding. Little by little, that sensitivity will awaken within you. The true goal of your exercises, even when they are aimed at a very precise object, is to lead you to the discovery of humanity and divinity. It is the path that will permit you to learn to accept in order to receive.

By performing these exercises, you give your body a priceless sense of well-being. Furthermore, if you practice the exercises frequently, your body will adopt them in its automatic responses and spare you suffering in the future, when you *believe* that your body suffers.

The Benefits of the Asana of the Beneficent Ocean

In this long inhalation movement, you have engaged in a great cleansing that has purified and oxygenated the blood. At the same time, this movement has relaxed and stretched the elevator muscles, the dilation of the viscera on the abdominal wall, and a deep lowering of the diaphragm. You have performed an internal massage by combining conscious inhalation and exhalation. During exhalation, you facilitated the elimination of nervous and muscular tensions. Your mental body focused on deepening your breathing. The work on your belly kept it sufficiently busy; it ceased to amplify the physical ache that it had taken on. So, the pain will be diminished by half or have disappeared completely.

The relaxation applied through your exhalation will awaken the senses. Your consciousness will perceive a renewed state of well-being and ask the mental body to enhance it further. This asana eliminates bellyaches, while promoting relaxation and well-being. It also eliminates constipation. It may make you feel a need to eliminate waste. Don't restrain yourself Moreover, it liberates the nervous tensions linked to anguish and anxiety. Your morale will return to a positive state, and your physical body will recover the sunbeams that light up its life.

Your body is in this world to adapt itself to all things with the sole goal of survival. It will rapidly understand the lesson; this exercise will be engraved in its physical and intellectual memories. You will only require a little bit of training to establish reference points for the body to which it will grow accustomed. Every time your body has the need, it will draw from this exercise of its own accord and will only call upon you later to help improve the effect. When it suffers another ache—a bellyache, for example—your body will no longer need you. The lesson will have been learned.

The more you perform the asana, the more your body will exceed limits that you thought it would never even reach. As you apply the fruits of this education, your body will offer the chance to discover new territories. It will become like a garden filled with flowers—where you take pleasure in breathing lungful after lungful of life's sweet perfume.

Since my earliest childhood, I have been fascinated by all living things. Like most children, I could never stop asking questions. The answers never seemed to satisfy me, because for every answer, I always formed another question. I have preserved this childlike thirst for knowledge. I would like to show you how to use it, in order to perfect your gaze and better nourish your being.

When the body feels you are depriving or abandoning it, the quality of its life declines. All of its innate gifts of adaptation and openness to knowledge are extinguished little by little, slowing its perceptive capacities as well as your own highest state of well-being and uplifting. You must prevent this from happening and cease to be deaf to its needs.

Do not limit the knowledge of your body to just the Asana of the Beneficent Ocean and to controlling stomachaches. It is your duty to listen to your body at every moment. It speaks to you constantly and sometimes calls out to you for help. It is seeking you out, and it needs to meet you. However, you will never be able to understand it, if you don't take the time to gaze at it through the mirror of the life that offers itself to you. From the surroundings of life, your physical body constantly receives vibrations that should guide you—if you know how to decipher them.

I urge this strongly. Above all, you must want it. Here's another idea: Study animals more closely. They serve as a mirror to interpret what comes from you.

THE LANGUAGE OF THE DOG

The dog wants to make you aware of the force of its love, the purity of its trust, and the depth of its state of well-being. It stands at your side and reflects the most beautiful experiences of life. Its body transmits sensations and feelings that make it capable of sharing life with you.

Even if you find it impossible to decipher the messages of animals, remember that your physical body is animal in nature—a radar detector that captures the sensory messages you often allow to be blown away with the wind. However, you are in this world to understand and develop these messages and your internal radar in order to attain your highest level of well-being.

Make some effort to pay attention. Seat yourself comfortably, close your eyes to facilitate solitude, and seek peace within yourself so you can relive experiences that remain in your physical and mental memories.

Look closely now at the dog. When it approaches you, it communicates sincerity through its body's quivering. It lifts its head with eyes fixed on you, tilts it slightly to the right, and lets you hear the panting of its exhalation. It stretches its neck a few inches forwards. By this gesture, it shows its concern for you, asking, "Are you all right?" Since you haven't answered its message, it repeats the same gesture by tilting the head to the other side, still expressing itself through its exhalation, and then straightens up. It touches you with its nose, as if to breathe you in better, to show you that you are the breath of its life. This gesture signifies, "I love you." If you are sitting down, it comes closer and caresses you with the tip of its nose, in order to affirm, "I am with you."

Since you are unable to decipher the dog's signals, you may think it just wants to be petted. It is not asking you for anything; it spends its life giving to you. It inhales deeply, and upon exhalation—the panting you hear so strongly—it rests its muzzle on your lap, or else lies down at your feet to confirm that it feels good being with you. This simple movement of exhalation sums up its state of feelings; "I love you, I'm happy to be with you, and with my breath, I caress you."

If you knew how to communicate through the vibrations of your body, you would have felt the echoes resonating from each of the dog's gestures or breathing movements. You would interpret these vibrations as sounds distinct from one another.

Like the dog's, your body transmits sounds according to what it receives from the life that surrounds it. If you listen, it will be possible to find yourself through these sounds. If you do not learn to gaze at the dog in order to understand it, you may never understand the being you should be.

When I was seven, I noticed my father, sitting in a tree in the forest, capturing birds that came to him. Amazed, I was unable to believe what I saw. I thought it was impossible to get closer than six feet to a wild bird and still less possible to capture one with my bare hands.

As part of my lessons, my father taught me how to do this. However, before I succeeded, it took me hours and hours of daily observation of the birds in the marshes, plains, and forests. I learned to interpret each of their poses and perform them with my own body, to guess their feelings, and explain them to my father. He taught me breathing and the appropriate poses so that, in each movement, the echo transmitted by my body would be just right. I could not be content to merely think; I had to *be*.

Throughout these months of research, my discoveries were so rich that I did not see time pass. I was time. Each day, my father told me, "If you want to capture the bird, you must become a bird yourself. Consequently, you must understand everything about him, so you can communicate to him what you want from him."

A bird guides itself only twenty percent by vision. In order to protect itself and find its bearings, it mainly uses the vibrations of its body. It sticks its tongue against its palate, dilates its throat, and opens its beak with a click to emit a sound. Then it orients its head, aligning its body to detect echoes of the sound it has emitted. I had to learn to emit the same sounds, send them off into the distance, then listen to my body receive their echoes. I repeated them over and over while remaining on the move. With my eyes closed, I had to describe all the surrounding forms to my father.

At the beginning, I caught different kinds of birds, just for practice. I had to be quick to place the captured bird inside my shirt, against my skin, to prevent it from seeing. To slow the beatings of its panicked heart, I would hold it against me, so that it could feel the pulse of my own heartbeats. I waited until it was completely calm before freeing it.

During these formative years, I came to understand that my body receives and transmits echoes of vibrations whose high, low, and medium frequencies depend on the objects and lives that surround me. From this, I have learned that those who content themselves with merely seeing forget to gaze in deep observation and remove themselves from the physical world by encouraging the regression of their physical bodies.

I am not asking you to learn how to capture birds with your bare hands. Nor am I asking you to converse with your dog—although these would be very enriching experiences. My goal is to awaken images inside you that will provide sufficient reason to educate and protect your precious body.

When I was a child, my father said to me many times, "If you want to understand the sea, look at the sky. Don't go searching in faraway countries for what, according to you, you lack today. Teach your body, and your body will teach you what you are seeking. And it is not always what you believe you are seeking."

Arouse within you the hunger and thirst to know yourself. Each day, allow this desire to nourish your ambition and sustain your willpower and in an obstinate way, so you will never encounter impatience or discouragement. Learn to become the time you will give your body.

CHAPTER 5

Channeling Energy: The First Steps Toward Meditation

Isolate yourself in your place of exercise. Remain standing barefoot for a few moments. Make sure that the soles of your feet are relaxed and flat on the ground, as though the earth was breathing through them. Breathe slowly but deeply: The two movements of breathing must be focused in the back of the throat (the Breathing of the Ocean).

Your arms should be relaxed at the sides of the body with the palms turned inward in a natural fashion. Now turn them in the same forward direction as the body. Your feet and your hands, which are perfectly relaxed, will become the essential elements that capture energy from the ground and the space around you, energy that you will feel in your body. While still standing upright, relax your body to permit yourself to feel the vibrations of the energies in movement better.

Your entire body is a radar detector that captures and transmits energy. You must remain attentive to it in order to feel the movements of energy through the feet and hands. You must never forget that the movements of exhalation naturally relax the body, and the pause after exhaling allows you to listen to the vibrations.

Preparing the Place for Seeking the Unity of Energy: Phase 1

For some time now, you have been gazing at the place you have chosen, and the feelings throughout your whole body invite you to listen to the place in order to melt into unity with it. Your body has been receiving the vibrations from the energy that surrounds it, like a little girl who wants to follow her older sister. Your inner gaze imprints itself on your being, which shivers like invisible tears of love; in your body, sobs begin to break forth. You feel your body waver, and you perceive this change across its surface. It has found its identity by discovering its link with nature (its yoga). It is experiencing the sensation of freedom. It is a part of nature, its older sister. You have only just met the body and it has opened the door to your path. Hands outstretched, the little sister opens her arms, imploring, "Take me with you into your space of liberty, so that I can build up the movement of life within me, so that my life regains its meaning and shows me the path of yoga."

You will undergo these states. You will believe you are living these emotions, and you are effectively receiving messages you don't understand. To cross this immense field that leads to birth, give your body intense consideration without confusing it with your mind. Learn to use the sensations your body transmits to you to encourage it to go further and gaze deeply in order to understand it.

After two or three minutes, start to move quietly. Try to walk only when inhaling and imagine that you are absorbing the ground through your feet. Do this until your lungs are full. Then pause with your lungs full. Don't ever forget that your body is the carrier of the senses. Breathing is the first link in the chain of life, and this inhalation lets you discover the depths of existence through the experience of movement.

Your body will feel a natural inclination to quit. Avoid feeling this way by supporting your body, strengthen the desire within it, and show it your presence by giving it what you are: love. Relax your facial muscles as much as possible, making sure the eye muscles are also totally relaxed. Lift your chin slightly to the wind so that your face can offer itself more easily to your chosen space, to the nature surrounding it and to the depths of your body's sensitivity. Your face must express the love and goodness that summons tolerance. It is your only path.

Before exhaling, stop all movement, making sure the relaxed soles of your feet are in full contact with the ground. Your goal is to strengthen your attention, deepen your gaze, listen and follow the feelings of your body without mixing them up.

Continue to remain motionless during exhalation. Eliminate any useless contractions from your body, and, as you exhale, imagine the ground beneath your feet drawing you in. Visualize someone making a light kiss with puckered lips and a recipient breathing it in the hope of experiencing it more.

The marriage of energies has started. Continue to breathe deeply. On each exhalation, try to relax in order to listen better. During each inhalation, feel your face lighting up more and more. Your eyes smile at life like a happy child's to permit your body, in its totality, to transmit the love that gives birth to the fluid sweetness and lightness of breath, its cloak of purity.

Help your body capture energy better and receive this energy in such a way that it snuggles up against you. Clothe yourself completely with the sensations of your body; they will facilitate communication and lead to knowledge. Imagine your body breathing energy through the palms of its hands and soles of its feet. Help it to become the radar that captures energy through its pores to transmit the inner light within you better. This light never shines on the person who does not know how to gaze inwardly.

Your preparation may provoke tears of purification as your body transmits the color of love's robe. Don't worry about this. These are not sobs; do not hold them back. Allow your body to wash away its hurt and lack of well-being.

When you are just starting, this preparation may be lengthy, but with practice, it will only take you two or three minutes. When I was a child, I devoted two or three hours to this seemingly simple preparation.

Don't become impatient running after time. It is imperative to understand this preparation in order to accomplish it with absolute success, because it will open the door to success in all of your sessions.

For this reason, do not enter the second phase too hastily under any circumstances. It is not vital to distinguish the two phases for your sessions to be a success. However, it is a choice you should make yourself.

Complete this phase by seeking the unfolding and the weightlessness of energies. Give your body the time to assimilate and execute what you are teaching it. Even if this preparation takes months of practice, wait for the body to become impregnated with it as an automatic response so that each subsequent exercise can really come alive for you.

Preparing the Place for Seeking the Unity of Energy: Phase 2

Once your place of exercise has become a part of you, start your session. By now, you are certain to understand fully the search for the unity of energy. It is not only performed by your body but truly lived by it.

From now on, walk by placing the tips of your toes on the ground first, then the whole length of your toes, the sole of your foot, and finally the heel. Do this only while inhaling and pausing. Inhale and take several steps. With each step, seek the lightness of your body's weight as if the ground you are inhaling is pushing you towards the sky.

At the pause, when your lungs are empty, stand so that the distance between your feet is equal to the width of your shoulders. During the pause with full lungs, continue walking as though a thread is attached to the top of your head and drawing you upward toward the sky. During inhalation and its pause, your body will become as light as a feather floating in the wind. Make the weight of your body disappear gradually while walking.

Stand still for two seconds while preparing yourself for the exhalation phase. While exhaling, stand squarely on the ground. As you exhale, place each foot down as a single block, sinking your body weight of your body into the floor to unite with it. The weight of your body should penetrate the ground.

Resume your walk. In this manner, walk in your place by guiding each of your steps so you listen better to the weight of your body and the energies allied with it. Let your arms freely express and interpret the sensations they experience.

Like the air that changes direction to accommodate the shape of a mountain or whirls through space like the nuptial dance of a butterfly, let your body float and dance with the energy that has united with it during your sessions. Never attempt to interpret the sensations and images that appear to you. That would be like closing a door that has opened to the light.

However, after each session, take the time to stop, gaze, listen and discover, because *a session that starts upon the path of Buddha never ends*. It is a gaze into the perpetual new beginning of life. It never stops.

THE PRANA THAT PREPARES YOU FOR MEDITATION: THE PRANAYAMA OF THE CHILD YOGI

Phase 1: The Seeking

With this pranayama, or controlled breathing, you begin the

education of your mental body, which will allow you to locate its opening later.

• Sit in a posture that is comfortable for you, with your spinal column as straight as possible.

• Place your hands on your knees in the energy-linkage mudra, turning the palms of your hands toward the sky and relaxing all your fingers. The tips of your thumb and the index finger should be joined to form a circle.

The Mudra of the Energy Link

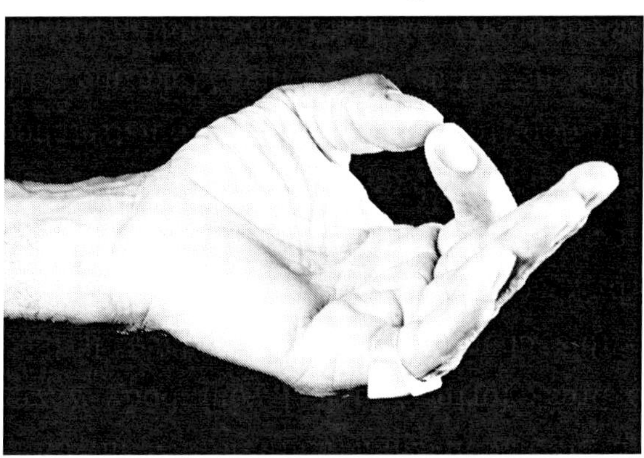

Figure 38

• Breathe slowly and very deeply.

• The two breathing movements should be focused in the back of the throat (Breathing of the Ocean). Relax your face, throat, and shoulders. In order to isolate yourself from external influences, make use of an exhalation to close your eyes. Direct them downward, without any contraction; your facial expression should remain neutral.

• To stabilize and support your mental body, observe your breath entering and exiting from your nostrils as if it has become visible. Don't try to interpret whatever forms or sensations reveal themselves to you; just satisfy yourself with watching them melt, build, and transform themselves inside you. Imagine you are breathing love. Let your breath express itself.

• Once you have found a regular rhythm in your breathing, become even more attentive to the feelings of your body. Your inhalations will awaken those feelings.

• Focus on the center of your palms and feel the presence of the energy and your body's breath, as if two crystal balls filled with light were placed on them. They are clearly present but also light as feathers. Use your exhalations to deposit energy in your hands while relaxing you. From this point on, the presence of energy in your hands will be more and more obvious with each inhalation.

• Visualize your body to make sure that the spinal column is very straight, right up to the cervical (neck) vertebrae.

This is your last glimpse of your internal state, before seeking the external aspects, and it is crucial. It will establish better interaction between your physical and mental bodies. When you resume, the development of your senses will be much stronger. You will create a more direct contact between the three aspects of unity: the being that you are (the mind existing in life), your physical body, and your mental body.

Once you have checked that your physical and mental bodies are ready, bring your mental body to the center of the pyramid formed by your hands. Now you can perform the Pranayama of the Child Yogi.

In this pranayama, each of the movements of breathing are extremely deep and carried out at the rear of the throat (Breathing of the Ocean). The inhalations are carried out in a continuous series of stages that change their flow every second. You must reproduce the effect of your dilating arteries with your throat. The sound of your breath represents the vital activity of your body, which will permit you to recognize your heartbeats, followed by the flow of blood. Count your own pulse and, after each beat, experience the echo of the flow of blood. Pause with your lungs full, for two to four seconds, to sustain your mental body, which is present in the echo of the just-completed breath. Imagine that you are continuing to inhale. Observe how the inhalation and its pause inform you of the very real quality of your inner state.

The moment of exhalation takes place in three stages, each of which lasts two seconds. Let your exhalation out calmly for two seconds, stop it for two seconds so you can listen to the relaxation of your body better, then exhale again for two seconds. You should always exhale by adapting yourself to your own rhythm, according to your breathing capacity, without expelling the last reserves of air that must remain in your lungs. Take two seconds to exhale, then two seconds to listen. The sound of your exhalation will send you the song of the ocean wave that approaches and lovingly embraces the shore with joy, then halts its surge for two seconds to call out and give you the pleasure of savoring its echo better before continuing to race forward.

At this point, you are ready to direct the gaze of your being on the fusion of the energy of your life and the surrounding world. This journey will carry you into the whirlwind of the dance of your new dimension.

Never forget that each posture and movement of your body has importance. Give yourself the time to try to understand the reason for each asana or posture. Perform them to learn to guide your body better and understand them in order to educate your body. You will never be able to offer your body something your mind has not acquired. Become curious and interested in nourishing your desire and become ambitious about your well-being and improving your life. This will give your body a life that is pure as a cloudless blue sky.

Your mental body will start to develop an observation of your physical state from the moment it unveils itself to you. This posture teaches you to suppress this automatic observation of your physical state by your conscious mind.

Try placing your body in the lotus posture—with your legs crossed and feet upturned and placed on the tops of your thighs. After a moment, the circulation in the lower part of your body will diminish more or less rapidly according to the degree to which you have taken care of your body. The knee and ankle joints will become painful, and your feet will grow cold and increasingly numb. At the very instant that your conscious mind takes note of this, your mental body will manifest the presence of suffering until it becomes unbearable. You are then incapable of continuing any breathing exercise.

By practicing this posture, you will first learn to prevent this awakening of consciousness that hampers your progress with its automatic responses. At the same time, you will train your physical body to become used to the stretching of the fibers in your joints. Little by little, your physical body will acquire the elasticity that it previously lacked. You will also find the comfort that will make you want to continue.

All of this serves to help you fully understand the respect and consideration you must bring to breathing. It will inspire you to concentrate and work on mental development before you meet the mental body itself.

This approach begins with a level of the mental body called the Level of the Image. It will help you draw on memories to build an image that will open you to feelings. Seek this image and make it live again during the movement of inhalation. Follow its evolution until the end of the pause with your lungs full. Then, during exhalation, penetrate into its real dimension. The pause following exhalation will give you the chance to listen to your body and to be with the energy that is taking form. As you breathe, withdraw from external activity to move beyond the automatic development of consciousness that forces you to remain aware of present sensations.

If you manage to achieve this state, you will attain the very first phase of supreme concentration, or *samadhi*. This will allow you to admire the internal dimension of your personal state and the path of the unity of energy that leads to the uplifting or the Higher Self.

Phase 2: Listening

Sitting comfortably in your posture, your relaxed face expresses peace, and the luminous smile of the Buddha awakens within you. Serenity begins to reign within your body, which is becoming your church, your temple of prayer.

Place your hands on your knees in the mudra that unites you to the energy that surrounds you. Breathe very slowly and deeply. Each inhalation will prompt you to find within your body the song of your heart that will mark its beat from the beginning of the inhalation. Afterward, you will receive an echo of the flow of blood that feels like a melody whose rhythm matches with the inhalation. In one inhalation under your control, nature finds its forms in order to give you an inner image of the wind that blows and the water that flows through the river at the center of your body. You have started to open the door of divinity that will reveal the child that sleeps within you; it will smile lovingly at you when it awakens.

Since your conscious mind no longer provides you with senses, you cannot become aware—you simply *become*. Since your eyes are exceeded by images that are beyond feelings, you no longer see with your outer eyes but observe the immense expanse of an inner state so beautiful that a happy child would weep with love. You have just received the key to the door of meditation.

Each exhalation will serve as a protective caress to your body and give it a feeling of ease. Exhale for two seconds, the amount of time needed for the ocean wave to lift and carry your body like a mother who holds a child at arms' length in order to better envelop it with her gaze. Suspend your breath for two seconds, allowing the force of love to bathe your body in vibrations and perceive the inner images that allow you to grow. By doing this, the body is transformed during exhalation and experiences what it truly is—pure energy. It is transported by the undulations of the waves to find its very base, its source, and to join with it.

Throughout the asana of the Pranayama of the Child Yogi, it will be possible to find the child within you and to gaze on it through your inhalations. Your joy will double when you feel that your exhalations permit you to listen to the inner child in order to appreciate it better. Just as the child is destined to grow up, he who enters this asana and attains the door of light (the samadhi) will re-emerge having grown in a way that serves humanity.

To attain, hold, and keep this state, your body is indispensable. You need it. You will never be able to breathe light if you don't educate your body. You must invest yourself passionately in its education so it responds to your passion religiously, so that it transmits the energy of the sun. Regardless of the degree of well-being it allows you to achieve, be willing to consider yourself ignorant. Then, you will grow even more.

During your hours of practice with the asana of the Pranayama of the Child Yogi, take into consideration the movement of the breath, which makes and supports the life of your body. Focus closely on it and stabilize it. With all your expectation and desire, let the force develop within you that will give you the form and color of energy in constant transformation according to the echoes and vibrations of your body.

Throughout the inhalation, and in rhythm with it, raise your hands to their original position so that all your energies unite. The sensations will communicate these energies to you internally through the movements of the asana to mark the elimination of the weight of your body, which becomes more and more noticeable. Always keep your elbows close to your body, with your arms bent, as though your two hands were sacred messengers bringing the energy to you as an offering. At the beginning, don't worry about the height you achieve with your hands. It may be your breathing capacity causes difficulties for you. This is normal because your body doesn't know how to breathe yet. Think of the child; before being able to walk on two legs, it crawls on its belly, knees, and elbows before one day learning the comfort of standing up. You will need to discover breath before learning how to breathe. Give yourself time, and your body will thank you for it.

During exhalation, in time with your breath, bring your hands back to their place. At each pause, gaze within. The movements of your hands must follow those of your breathing in a coordinated fashion and must stabilize themselves with each suspension of breath. The pauses will be physical, but the movements will continue mentally. The pauses following inhalation help to eliminate sensations of weight and height. The movements of your exhalations will be preceded by a moment of release, a more pronounced relaxation that will be interpreted by the body as a look of acceptance or a demand for profound communication. The pause in exhalation integrates these forms and movements. After several months, these movements of your hands to make mudras will simply become part of breathing.

You have been seeking the interaction of your mental body with the vital functions of your physical body to unveil new dimensions allowing you to gaze upon your body more deeply. Do you know the exact reason for adopting this approach? It is to find the purity that releases goodness through your body and to allow you to find the splendor of the love that is born of your being. Unfortunately, in this world, your body is the only means of diffusing the flash of love that lights up inside you. How can you let it transmit the light of your being if you don't accept it and are afraid of it, or you are afraid of others and what they may say of you?

From now on, accept your body, whatever its external appearance. Give it your love and your consideration with the depth of your being. Build your church within your body, and you will find your soul. You will transmit generosity to all who cross your path. You will transmit calm and goodness to those who speak to you. You will transmit love and fraternity to those who look at you and all those who desire it. You will show the light to those who desire it.

Even with all my desire and will, I will never be able to lead you to success, if you don't make the decision to accept your life so you can be free. Don't fall into modern civilization's trap that makes you believe that you must absolutely "succeed" in order to become acceptable to others. Apply yourself to your personal lessons, and you will succeed in life.

Phase 3: The Gaze, the Divine Source

You have reached the stage where the mere thought of seeking the child God that lies within you soothes you like a happy smile. You have found the path like the Buddha who closes his eyes to gaze at his profound being and receives the illumination he will one day transmit to his disciples. Day after day, your gaze will illuminate your surroundings. Yet it is not your life that will have changed but the gaze you bring to bear upon it. You will appreciate it—and grow.

Clothed in generosity and acceptance, you will be different in the eyes of others, You will hear their comments gladly without seeking to take advantage of them. One day, you will understand that it does not suffice to hear in order to receive. Months later, the echo of their voices will come back to you as images that animate themselves deep within you and transmit the reflection of what you are in the mirror. You must learn to gaze upon it in order to listen.

From now on, try to seek the mirror that will allow you to find the reasons for every event in life. To achieve this, educate your body to stop reacting hastily and spontaneously at every instant. It is your duty to help it learn to speak little and dispose yourself to listen, because each time your body intervenes without your consent, it intoxicates and blinds you. Don't ever forget that words and gestures are not always vital to understanding. Make use of your body to find the mirror within the other person that will transmit understanding of life to you. This is one of the first reasons for your presence in this world, even if not the most important.

The path of meditation will help your body eliminate its malaise and liberate you from a lack of well-being. Sitting everyday in your posture, devote yourself to the education of your bodies. Gaze with wonder on your mental body as it takes form in order for you to discover it, and your physical body as it interprets the moment so you may understand it. It is important that you never forget that, in all things, the physical body needs to adapt. Neither of your bodies could reveal themselves to you without the physical body. Their manifestation can only occur through it.

It will be your duty to give your body the opportunity to have pleasure and to desire this so that it can integrate your training into its automatic responses much more easily. Through this, it will adopt a way that will permit you to live fully. During each second of its life and each day of your existence, you will need one another. Walk with the physical body on the path of your truth. Promise yourself never to abandon it, because it needs you. Your physical body is indispensable to you and will remain so until the day it perishes.

Since you are still far from the stage of samadhi, you must continue to use your hands to give material existence to the forms and movements of energy that will appear to you one day. When it happens, you must be ready to focus on these forms so deeply that you welcome them into your center and give birth to the unity of the movement.

Close your eyes and assume your posture with your hands in the Mudra of Energy linkage, on either side of the body at the solar plexus, just below the sternum. Take some time to be in the movement of energy that swirls in the pyramid of your hands. Watch as it takes form very slowly, integrating with your body so that your sense of space and time changes.

With an inhalation, raise your hands above your shoulders while letting your bent elbows move away from your body slightly. Raise your hands to the height of your ears by following the rhythm of your inhalation but without pausing. Turn them, as if to form a semi-circle, so they are oriented in the same direction as your face. Don't forget to continue to visualize the movement of inhalation during the pause with full lungs. Watch as the energy that has been born in your hands develops and penetrates your two ears while uniting with your body.

During exhalation, your body will surrender itself further

and offer you the total freedom of its state. When the movement of exhalation starts, watch the energy turn slowly and become transformed as it envelops your form. The breath halts to integrate you with your body better, while your body is transformed in the following step.

From the beginning of exhalation, your hands will turn once again but this time in the opposite direction. Rigorously following your exhalation, lower your hands to their initial position, and stop at each pause in your breathing. By tracing the route of the energy with your moving hands, you will materialize the route. Your hands illustrate the forms and movements encountered in your inner space.

After a few months of practice, you will no longer need to trace the route taken by the energy with your hands. Your body will preserve the path that leads to the door of meditation in its memory.

From now on, you possess the key to the door of meditation. You will know when you arrive at the threshold of your inner space, also called the Higher Self, because every form, movement, and transformation will become you. You have no reason to become frightened, even if all this seems new to you: Everything arises from you and lies within you. You are simply embarking, consciously and deliberately, on the path that leads to the Higher Self. This is the beginning of the way that leads to the unity of God.

The key to knowledge and transformation lies in breathing. Consequently, your inhalation opens the door. Once it is open, you will know. But don't try to pass through the door, because you risk becoming lost. One doesn't penetrate inner space but rather becomes absorbed by it. You will perceive new, unfamiliar forms and colors coming toward you, like flashes of slow movements that wrap around you and transport you into your space. In reality, you are that space, and all your bodies are showing themselves to you.

The first body that will unveil itself and insist on always remaining present is the mental body. Its form, composed of seven interlinked spirals with seven different colors, will remain present to surround you and protect you. From this moment onward, you will leave behind the cocoon of the physical body.

You have voluntarily left behind the external world, the physical world in order to move toward inner space. It is possible for you to gaze on the mental body that radiates around the physical body, as it does normally in everyday life. By this path, you will one day find the door to the world of light, strength, and understanding.

THE POSTURE OF THE STUDENT

Take your mat and sit down on it with your two legs extended before you. Breathe very deeply, to make full use of the movement of inhalation. Assume the posture of the student by following these steps:

- Raise your arms above your head and expand your chest until the end of the pause in breath. Upon exhaling, bend your upper body over your legs, relaxing and stretching at the same time.

• During the next inhalation, straighten up the chest while moving the spinal column *in an improvised way,* in order to eliminate any contractions. This prepares the body to adopt its posture. This position is extremely valuable to inform the physical body that its cooperation will be demanded. Your left leg should remains extended and quite relaxed in front of you.

• Use an exhalation to bring the sole of your right foot as high

The Posture of the Student

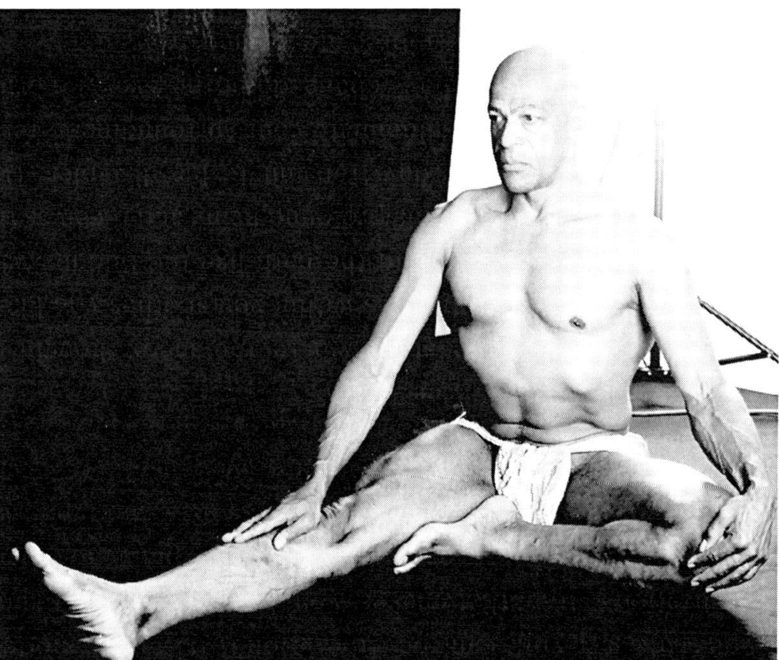

Figure 39

as possible up the inside of the left thigh. Keep your spine as straight as possible. Your buttocks should lie firmly on the floor.

• Place your hands on your right foot and left leg, palms turned up towards the sky. You can also place them on your legs, without taking into account the symbolism of the mudra.

The Posture of the Student closely resembles the Posture of the Young Adept. The only difference is that the back of the foot lies on top of the thigh with the sole turned to the sky in the Posture of the Student. When you see them, both of these postures look extremely easy and accessible to anyone. However, I advise you against entering any posture without preparation, to avoid the risk of bodily injury.

Make use of the asanas described below to prepare your body for its education and to give it the possibility of adopting its posture with ease and pleasure. The Posture of the Student prepares the body's joints for the asanas of forward flexing, such as the pincer, crab, spider, etc.

THE ASANA OF THE PINCER WITH BREATHING OF THE OCEAN

• Take up your starting position. Sit down with your legs lying extended before you and arms stretched at each side of the body. Place the backs of your hands on the floor.

• Focus your breathing in the back of your throat (Breathing of the Ocean). Breathe as slowly and deeply as possible. During inhalation, and in rhythm with it, raise your arms very slowly while keeping your fingertips pointed toward the sky (see figure 40).

• Once you have extended your arms above your head,

The Asana of the Pincer With Breathing of the Ocean

Figure 40

Figure 41

The Asana of the Pincer With Breathing of the Ocean

Figure 42

turn your hands towards each other (see figure 43). With arms bent, place your joined hands on top of your head.

• Once your inhalation is nearly complete, bring your elbows backward as far as possible.

• Pause four seconds with your lungs full.

• Stretch your entire spinal column throughout the pause.

THE ASANA OF THE PINCER

The goal of this asana is to prepare the body so it can achieve the ease required to adopt a posture and hold it for a period of time without experiencing difficulties.

• During the exhalation, tilt your pelvis forward so that your belly approaches your thighs (see figure 43). As you

Asana of the Pincer

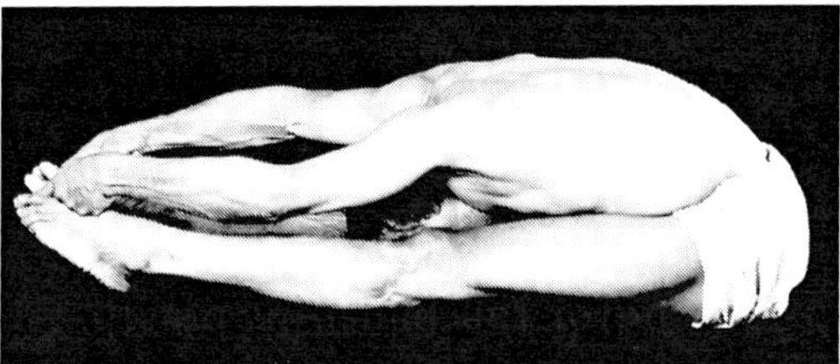

Figure 43

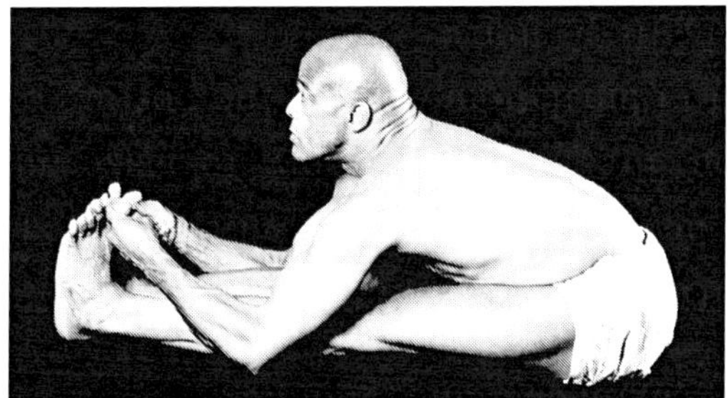

Figure 44

Figure 45

exhale slowly, continue to move your torso towards your legs.

• When you've flexed as far as you can, push on your arms to lengthen them. Lean on the backs of your legs in order to lift up your elbows, keeping your hands in place.

• Stretch your head towards your knees (see figure 44).

Keep your lungs empty for four seconds. Relax your pelvis and rear end fully.

• Maintain your position and inhale. Take hold of your legs and stretch your arms to bend them, pointing your elbows toward the floor.

• Lift your head as much as possible to lengthen the spinal column as far as possible (see figure 45).

• Relax your pelvis fully so that it can tilt forward easily. Hold this position for four seconds with lungs full.

• After exhaling, lower your head as much as possible, pushing on your arms to tilt your pelvis backward and rounding your back like a stretching cat.

• Hold your position with lungs empty for four seconds.

• Continue the cycle of your asana for three breaths. On the fourth breath, return to the rhythm of your inhalation.

• With your hands joined above your head and elbows back, stretch your spinal column, tilting the pelvis forward as far as possible.

• To exhale, lower your arms in the form of a cross then place the backs of your hands to either side of your body on the floor, as you did at the beginning.

• Perform the Breathing of Liberation four times before repeating the Asana of the Pincer four times.

Be careful! This is one of the most advanced phases of the Asana of the Pincer; you will not be able to achieve it at this level immediately. When you first attempt the asana, don't

The Closed Pincers Posture

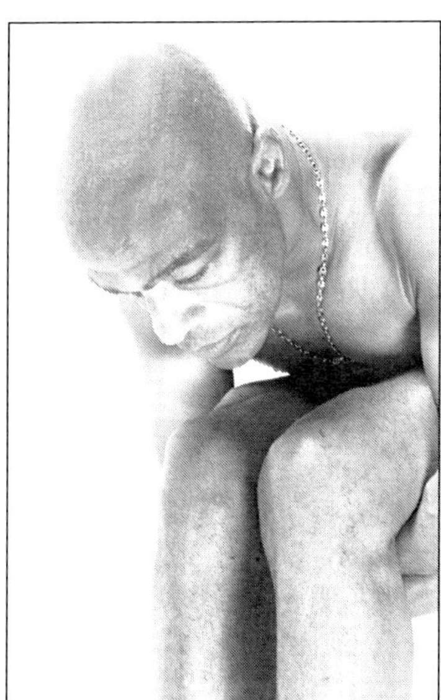

Figure 46

try to pass your hands under the soles of your feet or hold onto the big toes. Limit yourself to gripping your ankles, calves, or knees. The main thing is not to perform any supernatural feats but to regain the elasticity and comfort of your pelvis and spinal column.

ASANA OF THE HALF-PINCER WITH THE PRANAYAMA OF THE OCEAN

After several months of daily practice with the Asana of the Pincer, your body will have gained or recovered elasticity. This very noticeable comfort will arouse a need to achieve more. Move on the next higher stage with Asana of the Half-Pincer, but don't ever forget it is your duty to move at a gradual pace and not harm your body.

Asana of the Half-Pincer

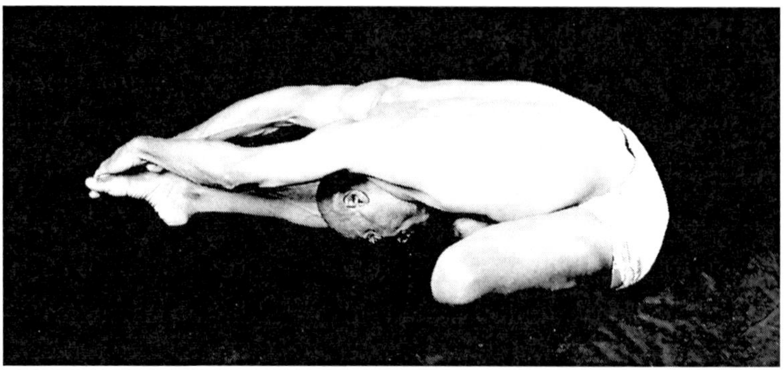

Figure 47

To carry out the Asana of the Half-Pincer, place your body in the Posture of the Student (see figure 39). Then, proceed exactly as in the previous exercise, the complete Pincer. Take care to switch to the other leg after each asana.

In the Asana of the Half-Pincer, the muscular stretches are much greater than in the Pincer. Don't rush into this, but give your body the time to acquire the gentleness required to transmit the goodness that will protect it. You will enjoy the beauty born of each of these movements. It is a very elegant asana that improves the elasticity of the muscles behind the legs, as well as the joints of the knees and ankles. However, it is fairly difficult to perform. You must take care to keep the pelvis as straight as possible so the spinal column remains aligned. Do this by keeping the two buttocks in contact with the floor.

When to Perform this Asana

This asana can be performed at any time of day.

Asana of the Half-Pincer

Figure 48

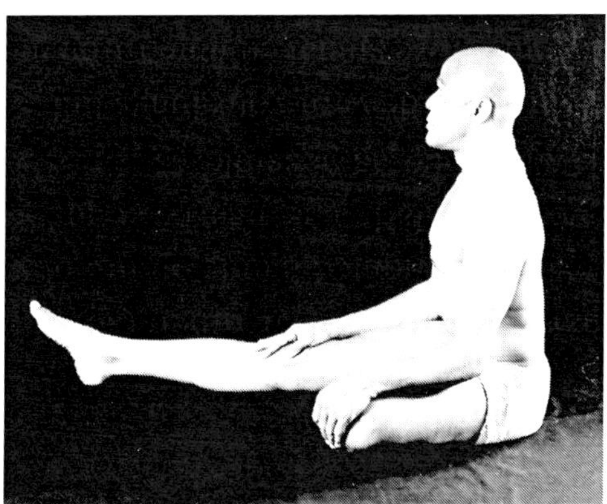

Figure 49

The Benefits of the Asana of the Half-Pincer

Thanks to this asana, your spinal column will be toned up and its elasticity improved. The same applies to your leg muscles (the abductors, femoral biceps, and calf muscles), plus the joints of the knees and ankles. These comforts will be welcome in everyday life.

Asana of the Saw

Figure 50

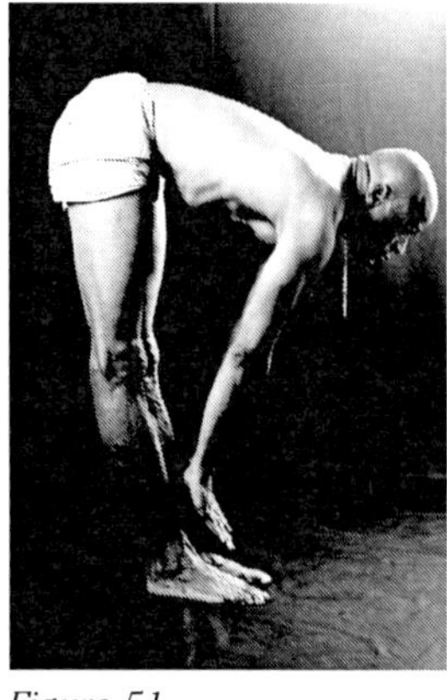

Figure 51

Figure 52

ASANA OF THE SAW

This is another asana that promotes elasticity. Consequently, exhalation has a more important role than inhalation.

• Stand up with your legs straight, keeping a hand's width between the feet. Place both hands on top of your knees.

• Inhaling deeply, push on your hands and tilt your pelvis backwards to stretch the dorsal vertebrae (opposite the heart) as much as possible, rounding your back like a cat. This first position is very important to feel the energy drainage along the spinal column (see figure 50).

• The movement of inhalation, which is powerful, takes place in a single flow at the rear of the nose, and develops within the upper thoracic cage. The inhalation can be considered as the return of the saw to its starting point.

• Upon exhaling, the saw bites into the wood deeply, then picks up speed.

• As you exhale, tilt your pelvis forward. This exhalation is carried out in two stages with an acceleration at the halfway point.

• During exhalation, let your hands slide down your tibia (lower legs) without touching them (see figure 51).

• Lower your hands and push on your belly to expel half the volume of air.

• When your fingertips reach the tops of your feet, flip your hands so the fingers point outward while quickening their movement to accompany the second phase of exhalation (see figure 52).

• Pause for two seconds.

• After the pause, exhale at the back of your nose.

• Return immediately to the starting position and then begin the asana again.

• Accelerate the movement while increasing its power in order to make the exhalation sing. The sound of your breath should closely resemble a saw working away on wood.

When you start out, spend ten to fifteen minutes per session working on this asana. During the asana, it is imperative to seek complete relaxation in the back of your legs, in order to allow the abductors and calf muscles to work easily.

Stand up straight from time to time in order to walk around and stretch the body, because the great ventilation from your breathing results in a purification of the blood that can cause a slight dizziness in some people (smokers, very nervous people, and those suffering from anxiety).

The Benefits of the Asana of the Saw

The Asana of the Saw is ideal to prepare the body for the training necessary to perform all the asanas and forward flexing postures correctly. Although its principal goal is seeking elasticity, it also eliminates nervous and muscular tensions and fatigue. It strengthens the muscles within the spinal grooves and improves the elasticity of the pelvis, the calf muscles, the abductors, and all the muscles along the back of the legs up to the buttocks. Thanks to better drainage of tension and an increase in respiratory capacity which purifies the blood, it regenerates the body.

ASANA OF THE INVERTED PINCER

This asana is performed with the Breathing of Vitality. The Breathing of Vitality is a very invigorating exercise with quick and brief but deep movements.

Continue to inhale through the rear of your nose into your upper chest, as in the Breathing of the Tree. However, at the end of this movement, attempt an abdominal contraction while straightening up your back. Exhale through the rear of the nose, as in the Breathing of the Ocean.

In the Breathing of Vitality, it is extremely important to perform all movements forcefully in order to facilitate the straightening of the lumbar vertebrae.

To perform the asana,

• Sit down, bend your legs, and plant the soles of your feet firmly on the floor.

• Pass your arms under your thighs in order to hold

Asana of the Inverted Pincer

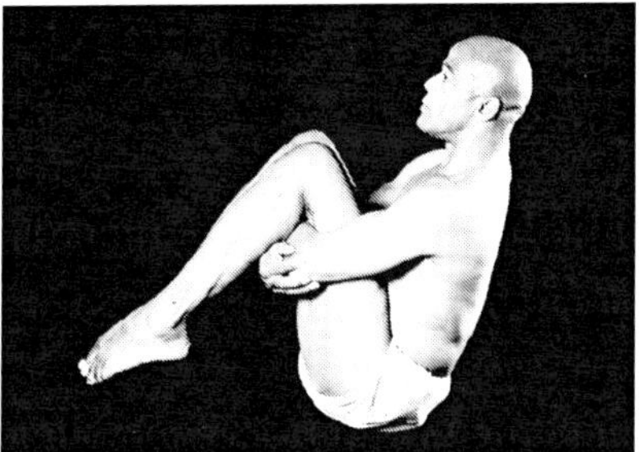

Figure 53

Figure 54

Figure 55

yourself by the elbows.

• Bring your thighs up and press them against your chest. Tilt your pelvis forward as far as possible in order to straighten the spinal column.

• Push on the tips of your toes while raising your heels to find your balance upon your buttocks (see figure 53).

• Inhale and tilt your body back slightly, so that your feet no longer touch the floor. Use your buttocks for balance. In order to do this successfully, always try to straighten up the lumbar vertebrae by pulling them inward, towards the thighs.

• As you inhale, raise your two joined legs as high as possible while hugging your thighs against your belly and chest and synchronizing the movement to your breathing.

• Keep your eyes focused on your toes.

• Pause for two seconds with your lungs full (see figure 55).

• As you exhale, bring your legs straight in front of you, with your knees making a right angle.

• Pause for two seconds with your lungs empty.

• In this manner, continue your asana for several rounds, still seeking perfect balance. Each breathing movement of your asana serves to straighten up your back as much as possible (see figure 55).

The Benefits of the Asana of the Inverted Pincer

This asana results in a purification of the blood through strong ventilation. It improves the dilation of the arteries and strengthens the muscles of the spinal column, especially in the vicinity of the lumbar vertebrae, which helps to prevent or relieve lumbago. It also enhances physical power and balance.

KATA OF THE CALL OF ENERGY

When I was a child, I almost always introduced the Kata of the Call of Energy into my sessions, because it immediately toned up the muscles involved. It gave me a feeling of power, volume, and lightness. This increased my endurance by helping my body avoid fatigue and adapt itself more easily to sessions lasting up to several hours.

This kata is truly extraordinary. It belongs to the family of spatial katas. Like all of the spatial katas and asanas, its real goal is to strengthen morale and nourish willpower.

This kata is often spectacular to watch but even more enjoyable to listen to, because it is accompanied by a particular type of breathing that you must take the time to learn. Don't let your mental body project the image of difficulty to you simply because the explanations might seem extraordinary. You must let the desire to carry out this exercise be born within you, to build the willpower to succeed. It will give you the desire to understand and to persevere. However, don't ask your body to start in haste if you're not sure you fully understand the breathing movement. Otherwise, you will be like a vehicle without lights that moves forward on an unfamiliar road.

For this reason, I offer first the appropriate breathing (the Pranayama of the Combatant).

THE PRANAYAMA OF THE COMBATANT

Adopt the Pose of the Combatant:

• Stand with your feet flat on the floor, toes pointing outward in the position of a pyramid. The distance between your feet should be four to eight inches greater than the width of your shoulders, with the legs straight but supple at the joints and your spinal column very straight.

• Hold your arms at the sides of your body and bend them

into right angles with the fingers very firm.

• Focus on a point on the floor more than two yards in front of you, and don't move your eyes away from it. This is your energy and focal point.

• Relax all your facial muscles. Only your eyes should focus on and absorb the point you have chosen, because all the energy in your body will be born from this point. At the same time, consider it a danger, like a snake you must hypnotize in order to prevent it from striking, an enemy you must empty of its force so it cannot attack.

• Inhale deeply through the rear of your nose and your upper chest. At the beginning of the inhalation, your nasal passages should be normal, but at the end, you must dilate them completely so that abundant air can enter suddenly and strongly before stopping short. The sound of your inhalation should resemble a whip slashing the air and whistling in the wind, before cracking against its target.

• Remain in place during a pause of two to four seconds with your lungs full.

• Exhalation takes place in two movements. Begin at the back of the throat. With an abdominal contraction, expel the air powerfully through your nostrils.

• At the end of the exhalation, increase the force of your breath, which leaves by the mouth and emits a sound of relief, before stopping abruptly.

• The sound should resemble the hissing of a menacing snake. To make that sound, clench your teeth with your mouth almost closed and leave a small space in front to expel the breath powerfully.

- It is imperative to be able to hear the sound of your breath loudly. This serves to motivate you and awaken the energetic capacity of your body.
- Pause for two to four seconds with lungs empty before starting over.

THE KATA OF THE CALL OF ENERGY AND THE PRANAYAMA OF THE COMBATANT

While performing this breathing, try to understand its distribution and diffusion within your body. To channel your energy, exercise your muscles. During the movement of inhalation, and in time with it, you only need to spread all of your fingers wide and just barely flex your knees so that your body can awaken instinctively like an animal placing itself on guard. You will feel a contraction that will be more and more noticeable in the pectorals, forearms, biceps, and triceps. This contraction will be spontaneous and automatic. You should encourage it in order to observe it better.

Hold this position until the end of the pause with your lungs full. At the moment of exhalation, return your legs to their initial, straight position. Bend your fingers to form the claws of an animal on the defensive before opening again with the next inhalation. Inhalation takes place for two to four seconds, with a pause of two to four seconds, followed by an exhalation of two to four seconds, and another pause of two to four seconds.

Kata of the Call of Energy with the Pranayama of the Combatant

Figure 56

Figure 57

Benefits of the Pranayama of the Combatant

The Pranayama of the Combatant is a natural stimulant, which is extremely effective against fatigue. It improves circulation, and in men, invigorates sexuality.

THE KATA OF THE CALL OF ENERGY

Once you think you have educated your body sufficiently by performing the Pranayama of the Combatant, you are ready to coordinate the kata with the pranayama. Keep in mind that the movements of the kata must be synchronized perfectly with the breathing to achieve unity in all aspects.

- With your arms at each side of the body, start your breathing. Make use of your energy points in your hands, arms, pectorals, and thighs to channel the energy in your

Kata of the Call of Energy with the Pranayama of the Combatant

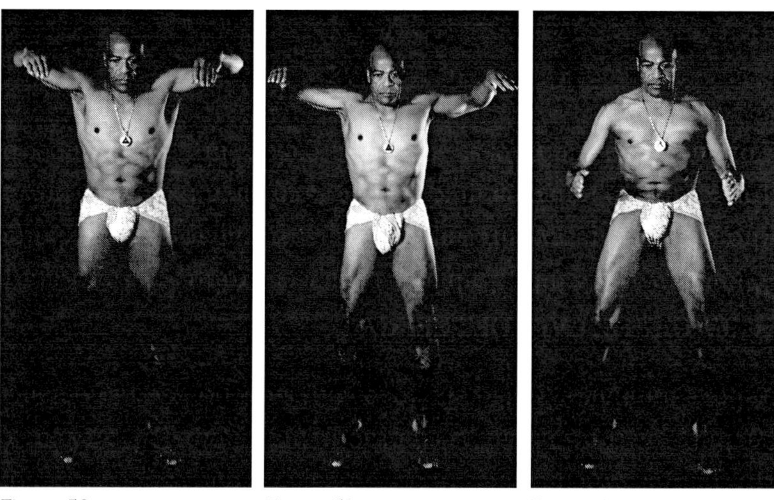

Figure 58 *Figure 59* *Figure 60*

body (see figure 56). Keep your forearms parallel and bent almost at right angles. Your thumbs and fingers should held tightly against one another, so that your hands become defensive weapons (see figure 57).

• Focus on the point of energy you have chosen on the floor.

• At the start of the inhalation, turn your palms toward the floor. Bring them forward and raise them so that your arms are extended at an eighty-degree angle. At the same time, raise the shoulders (see figure 58). Once you have lifted your arms to the height of your ears, your elbows should be brought back as far as possible (see figure 59). When your hands reach your ears, lower them with the palms turned inward to the level of your waist and bring them closer to the body.

• In a synchronized fashion with the hands, lift your heels

from the floor and bend your knees slightly to adopt the Pose of the Combatant and achieve a maximum contraction in a minimal amount of time. If you experience difficulty in maintaining the balance of your physical body while standing on the tips of your toes, concentrate on the point of energy in front of you. Your body will recover its balance spontaneously.

• Maintain the kata and the suspension of breath for two seconds.

• During the first phase of exhalation, return your heels to the floor and straighten up your legs. In the second phase, exhale through your mouth with fingers spread and bent into the form of claws. Draw your hands together with resistance as though they are hindered by an imaginary force.

• During the two seconds' pause with lungs empty, return your hands to the opening position.

• After a cycle of ten katas, take a pause to perform three Asanas of Liberation. Then you can start over, if you feel the desire.

• Modify your inhalation in the second stage (increasing the volume of the final inhalation). Accelerate the movement of your hands at each side of the waist toward an imaginary target. End the movement and the inhalation with a sudden clap (see figure 61).

In the Kata of the Call of Energy, each time that you point forward with your two hands, in rhythm with your inhalation, you will plug in your body to the point of energy in order to transmit the sparks of its power. Since the physical body always needs external support, it is important to hear the sound of your breathing. This point of stimulation will carry the body off in an intoxicating whirlwind that will multiply its power.

Continue to increase your training and give yourself time to understand, so that your body learns to join you in the experience of the asana. You must achieve unity in all respects with your asana—in the movements of the body, the breath and your visualization, so that the senses can transmit the inner dimension to you during the movement and allow you to discover the true evolution of your body.

When to Perform this Kata

Avoid performing this in the evening, since you would risk upsetting the natural cycle of sleep.

The Benefits of the Kata of the Call of Energy

This asana strengthens and develops the major pectoral, deltoid, bicep, quadricep, latissimus dorsal, trapezius, and calf muscles as well as the Achilles' tendons. It channels energy through the whole of the body while strengthening and stimulating the morale. It also facilitates concentration and physical balance.

To ensure obtaining benefits from this kata, it is imperative to work not only on the development and strengthening of the physical body, but also on the education of the mental body—a partner that you must never neglect. In all things, you must always consider the mental body as the guardian that holds the key to the door of success. Desire causes your mental body to appear, but when your mental body opens its door, it gives birth to a morale that will always remain very important. You can call it the path of truth, because the appearance of morale opens a road for you. If you make an effort to give your mental body healthy input, it will give birth to a positive morale that will clear your way. You will advance with joy, strength, and serenity on a path of light, until you meet with success.

Morale is a level of being that belongs to the mental body but constantly influences the state and the behavior of the physical body. It's important to obtain the means to permit your mental body to build positive morale in all circumstances so that the truth of your life will always bring you satisfaction. If you let your mental body nourish itself with blurred images full of doubts and lack of confidence, it will weaken your morale and overwhelm you with uncertainty. You will spend a great part of your life navigating fog-bound heavy seas in an unsafe boat without a rudder. You will be caught up in the vicious circle of the repetitive patterns.

To guarantee the development of positive morale capable of ensuring that you live in freedom and harmony, you must learn how to breathe. Through breath, you can gaze upon the evolution of energy, the source of the feelings that stimulate your senses. You will give yourself greater willpower to nourish your desire. The key to opening your door of truth lies in your desire; its use will draw from your willpower.

In most of the asanas, katas, and aerial postures, your seeking will be based on the point of your truth—the building of positive morale that transmits the real, personal dimension.

PREPARATION OF THE KATA OF LIGHTNING WITH THE PRANAYAMA OF THE ENERGIZED YOGI

The Kata of Lightning is a tremendous kata of muscular reinforcement. Before starting, it is advisable to train yourself to harness your breath perfectly with the Pranayama of the Energized Yogi. Without this breath, your kata will lose all of the virtues that make it worthwhile.

THE PRANAYAMA OF THE ENERGIZED YOGI

• Stand up, keeping a distance of about twenty inches between your feet.

• Lift your arms, bend your elbows, and lift your hands straight up in the direction of your gaze towards a fixed point on the floor, your point of energy.

• Bend all of your fingers in the shape of claws and point the tips toward the sky.

• Finish by moving your hands as far back as possible, at the height of the shoulders, with a space of four to eight inches separating them from each shoulder. This will support the straightening and strengthening of the muscles in the spinal groove.

You are now in the ideal position to begin the Pranayama of the Energized Yogi.

• While keeping your hands in the same position and making sure they maintain their initial height, extend your arms at a ninety-degree angle.

• Focus on your point of light, because you are going to

draw from it the energy required to strengthen and develop your physical body and your morale.

• At the beginning, your point of light will be indispensable to maintaining your mental body in a state of readiness: Its first goal is to keep the images of thought that are unrelated to your seeking away from your mental body and to obtain the the harmony needed for its education.

• While inhaling forcefully through the rear of your nose, bring your hands a quarter of the way toward you and accentuate the bends in your fingers. At the same time, bend your knees a quarter of the way.

• Pause for one or two seconds.

• Inhale again.

• Bring your hands back by another quarter, still accentuating the bend in the fingers and the straightening of the chest.

• After a one- or two-second pause, inhale one final time.

• Return your hands to their initial position as far as possible, straightening up you torso and lifting your chest.

• Pause for three to six seconds and lower your hands to the level of your chest with your palms turned toward each other as if you were going to flatten some imaginary object.

• To foster the energy that invigorates your body with each inhalation, imagine you are drawing the point of light towards you in order to absorb it totally. Consider that each inhalation naturally results in an accumulation of energy, and your role is to permit your body to receive it correctly.

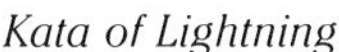

Kata of Lightning

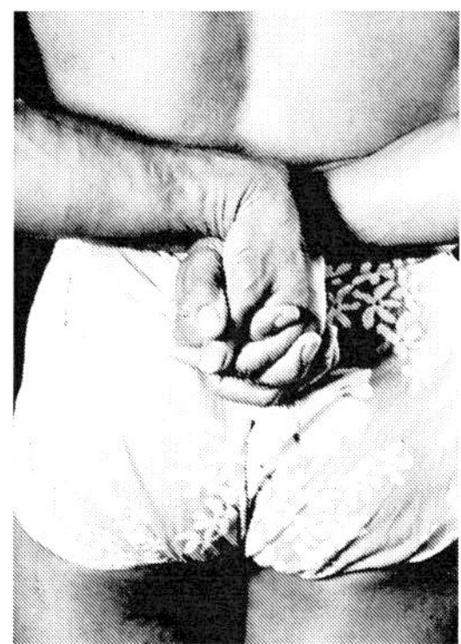

Figure 61

• The sound of each inhalation should resemble the whistling of a whip as it splits the air or the whistling of point of a flexible sword before it reaches its target.

• In time with exhaling from your abdomen, which takes place in a single movement, bring the palm of your left hand up to your chest.

• Push against an imaginary wall located in front of you with the palm of your right hand.

• Keeping the same rhythm, straighten your legs with force to return them to the original position.

• Although the Pranayama of the Yogi is channeled solely through the nostrils, the sound of the exhalation can resemble the cry a kung-fu master emits when gathering his energy during an attack.

The Benefits of the Pranayama of the Energized Yogi

At each pause, take note of your increased power and strength, as the exhalation gives you the satisfaction of being in harmony with your body.

Kata of Lightning

Figure 62

Figure 63

This breathing exercise helps to build a positive, strengthened sense of morale. It stimulates the brain and memory, improves automatic coordination, regulates the heartbeat, helps arterial dilation, increases the respiratory capacity, aids pulmonary ventilation, and strengthens the muscles (the pectorals, the rib muscles, and the deltoids).

THE KATA OF LIGHTNING

The Kata of Lightning uses the Pranayama of the Energized Yogi. Be sure you keep the importance of your point of light in mind, because it is essential to carry out this kata.

To begin, stand with your legs and spinal column as straight as possible, and your feet ten to eighteen inches apart. Join your hands and cross them at the back, with your left hand on the right and the right hand on the left, the fingers intertwined and pointed downward.

- Bend your elbows and raise your hands to the height of the first lumbar vertebra (see figure 61).
- While inhaling, lift your right leg to place it at a right angle to the rest of the body, pointing the toes forward (see figure 62).
- After a one-second pause, begin a second inhalation.
- At the same time, bend your leg while keeping your thigh horizontal and your toes pointed at the floor.
- Pause again for a second (see figure 63).
- Carry out a third inhalation.
- Raise your leg again to a right angle, taking care to synchronize the movements of the leg with the breathing.
- Pause for a second.
- Keep your leg stretched during the pause with your lungs full.
- Before lowering your leg to the floor, harden the muscles and lift the foot, so that the toes point toward the sky.
- Lower your leg, keeping it quite straight. At the same time, lower your hands, which are still linked behind your back, as low as possible on the buttocks.
- Exhale once your feet are completely flat on the floor, one beside the other. Pause for three seconds.
- Repeat the previous steps with the other leg. Don't forget to raise your hands before inhaling and to lower them along with the leg.

Throughout your kata, take care that the spinal column is kept as straight as possible. The position of your hands at your back should help you to do this. Make sure that they firmly rest upon the first lumbar. The position of the spinal column is very important. When lowering the hands following exhalation, go as far as you can in order to facilitate the relaxation of the shoulders and to perfect the straightening of the dorsal vertebrae (opposite the heart).

This kata should always be carried out in a dynamic fashion while maintaining a reasonable rhythm adapted to the body's capacities.

The Benefits of the Kata of Lightning

This kata augments pulmonary capacity and encourages muscular strengthening and development in the thighs, calves, inner legs, buttocks, the oblique and lumbar muscles. The joints in the knees, ankles, hands, wrists, and shoulders are also strengthened, which helps to halt the growth of rheumatic problems. It improves the balance of the physical body.

I have given you what you need so that your physical body will always want to be with you. These are the means of allowing it to take great pleasure from your practice, so that that you will always look forward happily to these daily training sessions. I want your physical body to gain a sufficient state of good health so that it can suggest to the mental body that it follow its example, in order to build the ally of positive morale. This will generate willpower within you, the force that nourishes ambitions.

Give yourself the means so that in every life situation you no longer have to submit with your body but so that you control it as you educate it. Live fully in the freedom and fulfillment you have regained, as freely as on the first day of your life. Recover this liberty in the clarity of the movement of life within your body. Read how it functions and follow its reactions like a father who opens the doors of the house wide to listen to his child. Gaze through the images of your mental body, beyond mere sight, and don't submit to them. Be sufficiently disposed to receive them, like a picture upon which the teaching of life is painted and which you draw over again in order to discover its depth. Gaze at life with love and tolerance, and accept everything in this world to arrive at knowledge.

HOW TO PREVENT ANGER

Find the incentive never to become angry again or suffer from the nervousness that all too often descends on your body like a great veil of hatred, impregnating it and disturbing your house.

Why should you forbid your body from becoming angry? Anger diminishes the quality of life and reduces its duration. Each moment of anger modifies your external appearance by aging your body, and your faith in the body fades little by little, diminishing your force and consideration.

Your body is your vehicle, the witness of your life and activity. It reflects the life that surrounds it and the sensations it experiences, so that you may understand your body with the goal of meeting your self.

Your body also emits radar. When it manifests anger that escapes your control, it shows your incapacity, impotence, and ignorance. Since you do not understand the message, your body loses its bearings. It no longer has any support and can only hang onto the gazes of those you have just shocked; the suffering is reflected by those who love you. These images will remain inscribed in your body's physical and mental memories. The next time, you will make use of them to improve your understanding of what nourishes anger—which is almost always born of ignorance.

Whatever the cause that provokes your anger, you will always have a choice. You can let it destroy you along with your body, or consider it as a message that needs to be interpreted.

Before letting anger invade you, seek within its cause the reasons that should nourish your will to walk the path of the Buddha, the acceptance of the act, and the wisdom that will allow you to remain in the light. Find these reasons through two scenarios:

1) You become angry, you say things you don't believe, you act or react in ways you you don't want, and your lost, defenseless body, which is drunk with your ignorance, becomes an individual who was hitherto a stranger. It suffers in the flesh and with all your being; deep inside, you are crying. The worst thing is, you have lost friends and made enemies, perhaps aggravating the root cause along the way. A malevolent sense takes hold that may last for years without it ever being resolved. You realize that this destructive anger

has not permitted you to find a solution, since it has not advanced your affairs.

2) You don't get angry, you control your breathing and soften your face through relaxation, and you are attentive to your body in order to remain at peace. You gaze at the person before you with respect, letting your body transmit your goodness, comprehension, tolerance, and acceptance. By doing so, you open a door of communication that will calm the person with whom you are speaking and facilitate a favorable exchange between you. While insisting on obtaining what you want, your body will transmit what you have always been—love.

It may be that neither of these solutions resolves your difficulties. However, choosing the second scenario will remain the more favorable course of action for you. You will not commit an act of aggression against your body or diminish its life, but you will gaze upon it and communicate with it. The most important thing, in my eyes, is that you will have profited from this situation to find in the other person the mirror that transmits the reflection of the foolish behavior you must no longer permit. You'll do this without making judgments about him or her. Accept that aggressive behavior, bad faith, and simple meanness born of ignorance is not, like all things in life, the result of chance. It is a message intended to improve you. Never pass up an opportunity to gaze upon, listen to, and breathe life with your body, because it is your guide.

The person who has taken aggressive action toward you and consciously wants to do you harm is, in reality, bringing you the good that is lacking in his or her being. Without knowing it, the person is living an unbearable state of negativity and asking you for help. One of the only ways to help him is the second scenario.

When the vehicle of the body grows angry, it shows signs well beforehand. The temperature of your body will be modified. The contractions and relaxations of your breath will transmit sensations to you (differences in temperature, stinging, superficial or deeper trembling, irregular sweating). Because respiration is the first link that becomes modified, your voice will be deformed. Your disjointed words may make a phrase inaudible. There are many other signs as well. If these do not suffice as warnings, you are far from your path. Always be aware of the state of the body, and you will observe these signs before the undesirable anger occurs,

Make the decision to prevent anger and stick to it. It lies within your power. It is up to you to draw from your desire the necessary force to acquire willpower. The health, quality, and duration of your life depend on it.

There is no better way to educate your body to stop submitting to the reasons that generate anger than the art of breathing. Train yourself with the Breathing of the Ocean. It is a tremendous regulator and regenerator of the body.

It is not necessary for you to isolate yourself to do this. On the contrary, take advantage of opportunities to go outside, adapt your breathing to each thing in your everyday life, and preserve a constant link with your body. To teach the body to lead a new life of peace, serenity, tolerance, and love, instill what I have given you by adapting it to ordinary circumstances.

When you are walking, avoid the haste of someone in a hurry. Walk calmly. Breathe deeply as often as possible, always with the Breathing of the Ocean. With the Breathing of the Ocean, count the number of steps needed to fill your lungs. Consider each burst of energy as an opportunity, a treasure invading your body with happiness. At the end of the inhalation, give your body time—about two seconds—to enjoy the quality of the breath with which it has just nourished itself.

Each time you do this, try to hear the sound of your breathing clearly, even while walking. Your body will interpret the sound as a beneficial melody that guides you towards peace. In its collective memory, your body will seek the tranquil image transmitted by the ocean. This will help it banish the haste of its spontaneous reactions that encourage nervousness and cause anger.

Similarly, during exhalation, count the number of steps necessary to empty your lungs but without using up their reserves. Take advantage of this moment of exhalation to relax your body by loosening your facial and abdominal muscles. When these body parts are controlled and relaxed, the others will follow. Your body will understand what you expect of it and its automatic responses will continue what you have begun. Even if your daily movements don't exceed a hundred yards or five minutes of walking, you will still teach your body and facilitate the elimination of nervous and muscular tensions.

From now on, when you must speak to someone, do it with the Breathing of the Ocean. Take the time to inhale deeply without the other person hearing the sound of your breathing. You should only use the movements of exhalation to form your sentences. Exhalation should take place through your mouth and serve to shape your words. As you exhale, take care that the pitch of your voice is never high but even-pitched or as low as possible without being muffled. To help make your voice calm and serene, your exhalations should be abdominal, with your throat and vocal cords relaxed, and your face peaceful. You should always choose the end of a sentence to terminate the exhalation, keeping the mouth closed in order to begin inhalation calmly.

From time to time, during the conversation, pause long enough to breathe very deeply, as if sighing. The person with whom you are speaking should see it clearly. This simple breathing movement will express tranquility and unconsciously cause the other person to relax. The serenity you establish will enable the other person to listen to you with greater pleasure and without worrying about the passing time.

Suppose you are in the middle of eating too quickly, in a way that hampers the life of your body. You become increasingly breathless, and you gain weight and lose body tone because your body's surface fat fills with more liquid each day. Unfortunately, because the body has a tendency to adapt itself and grow accustomed to everything, you are deliberately allowing it to destroy itself.

Starting now, adopt the Breathing of the Ocean, even while eating. Avoid talking too much or doing anything else at the same time. Really devote this precious moment for your body to chew your food thoroughly without omitting abdominal stretching, as I explained in my previous book *Body Agreement.*

Imagine you are face-to-face with someone whose behavior is such that it could arouse anger within you. A few months ago, this situation would have destabilized you. Today, savor this moment to apply what you have been teaching your body. Try to guide its serenity by performing the Breathing of the Ocean. Upon each inhalation, relax the muscles of your face so that it transmits the sun that is born of your being and your gaze reveals the purity that erases all judgment. Upon each exhalation, watch your belly relax while you concentrate on listening. In this way, you will govern the breathing of your body, where previously it would have submitted to the influence of the life that surrounds it.

Since your body has radar that detects signals and a mirror that transmits the reflections, other people will unconsciously perceive your attention, your efforts to listen, your consideration and respect. Without knowing it, you will be transmitting to them everything you have given your body. They will appreciate it greatly and even make a bigger mistake by thinking that they appreciate you. In reality, what they appreciate is the calm transmitted by your body that causes their own to be soothed.

Confidence will strengthen the willpower within you and provide the means to follow your own path more intensely and advance with greater precision towards the unity of life. It's up to you to make use of it.

From now on, don't be a wandering child without any bearings who clings to anger like a lifebuoy and drowns with it. Make use of every instant to understand your life. Don't become poisoned by the anxiety that comes from the ignorance of a misunderstood life. Always walk side by side with life, attentive to your body's gaze in order to understand its feelings and read its memories.

Even during a simple conversation in which your body has the habit of getting carried away in interpreting your impressions, give it the time to wait and give yourself the time to listen. Before saying a word, ask yourself, is this indispensable?

If your answer is yes, ask yourself if it's urgent. If your answer is still yes, seek out why the matter is so urgent and vital. During this moment of examination, you will understand that the person who does not speak or says little always faces a mirror that reflects and informs about life.

You will also understand that in this world, the essential qualities are found where you want them to be. It still doesn't mean they are reality. Urgency is often born from that which you believe to be essential but which only serves to feed your anxieties.

By following this teaching, you will learn to listen to others in order to better gaze at yourself, and you will authorize your body to transmit harmonious vibrations. The majority of those who approach you will have the pleasure of immersing themselves in a sweet and comfortable moment. You will elicit their sympathy. Since your body will still be playing the role of detector, it will translate the interest towards you into positive vibrations that will strengthen your confidence. However, you must take care not to stray from your road by considering yourself a generous fool. Never forget that the person who listens is the one who receives. Let your body adopt the Breathing of the Ocean for all occasions. At some point, your body will surprise you by performing it as an automatic response to enhance its comfort and facilitates its freedom. In this way, it will keep you on the path of wisdom.

Become the child that walks in the tracks of Buddha, so that the serenity you regain brings assurance and precision. May your path always be enlightened.

MEETING THE MENTAL BODY: LEARNING TO LEAVE THE PHYSICAL BODY

Step by step, we have advanced toward the knowledge of our physical bodies so that we can understand how they function and aid us in our lives. Your body is the crudest but most beautiful manifestation of your existence. If you persist in neglecting your knowledge of how it functions and ignoring the quality of its life, it will never be possible to meet your self.

It is often the case that your first body, the physical, is the least important of your bodies. However, it is essential for life, knowledge, existence, and the attainment of supreme well-being. When you speak of it, you permit your self to say, "Me" or "I". Me is not the Higher Self. But it does carry the Higher Self. It is not the self, but the Higher Self lies within it.

Throughout its life, at each manifestation, it calls upon your second body, the mental body, to help interpret and awaken your intuitions. Unfortunately, these two bodies have a tendency to become mixed up far too often. They completely scramble the experience your physical body should take from life in order to raise it up as the main source from which you will draw the knowledge that leads to well-being.

I want you to be positive at all times. By permitting yourself to separate from your physical body and encounter the mental body, you give yourself the possibility of no longer confusing thought and desire. As I wrote in *Body Agreement*, thought often remains just an image, an idea without an action that exhausts morale. Thought gives birth to desire but does not nourish it.

The mental body will decode the messages of life that your physical body transmits. You should learn to discern what flows from one body to the other and have the good fortune and the power to find your authentic self one day. Separate yourself from your physical body to encounter the mental body.

Throughout your whole life, you have seen your mental body as a visiting stranger. I want to teach you to gaze upon it and understand it, in order to protect yourself and strengthen it. Stop allowing the mental body to come to you automatically, at any instant, and trouble you with stray thoughts that come and go at the whim of any movement.

The mental body is not located within the physical body. Like circles that radiate around it, it nourishes itself from the physical body. The knowledge of both these bodies is indispensable to your education and supreme well-being. When the door to your inner space is opened, you will feel a sense of liberation in your being—a lightness and sweet freshness in your body that envelopes and clothes you in a breath of love. Your physical body will become your vehicle and your path. You will possess a little glow to orient and guide your steps to the highest state of well-being.

Desire creates willpower in order to attain its goal. It nourishes itself with inner focus, feelings, and satisfaction, from which are born strength, light, and knowledge. In order to meet your mental body, you must move toward it. For that to happen, it is imperative to come out of the physical body. You must hold yourself above it.

Keep these three key words of meditation within you forever: "before," "learn," "together" (BLT). "Before" coming to yourself, you must discover, esteem, and nourish yourself from your bodies. "Learn" to gaze upon them, to caress them by breathing in order to tame them. "Together" with them, find

The Diamond Posture

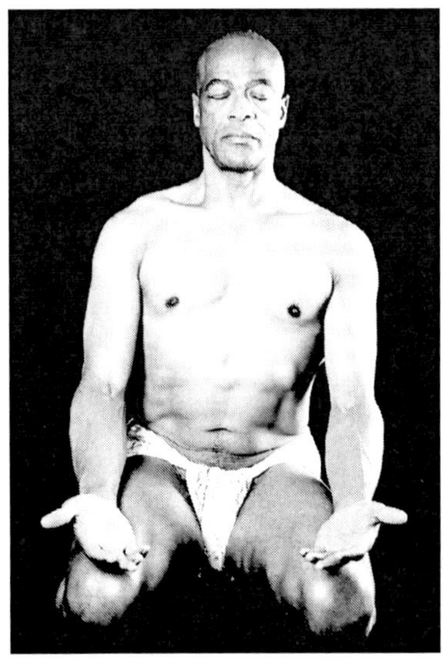

Figure 64

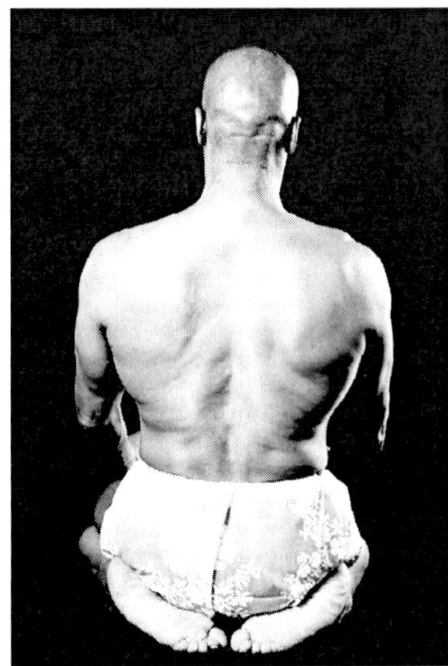

Figure 65

the unity and harmony that give rise to joy and desire. Give yourself the strength to succeed. Don't stop on your way. Adopt the Diamond Posture (described below) or any other posture within your reach, as long as it's comfortable. You can even exercise lying on your back. Don't ever cause aggression to your body. However, whatever the position, your spinal column must always remain as straight as possible.

Your first steps will focus on mental stability. For many people, keeping the mental body focused on a single thing for several minutes without any thought seems impossible. Yet this will help you perfect yourself. Make use of your physical body as a vehicle and path. The first two links in its life are breath and vibrations. These are your guides to following the mental body. Observing the movement of breath permits you to stabilize the mental body. From your desire, draw the patience that you will offer to your body.

THE DIAMOND POSTURE

The Diamond Posture is very simple to perform, and it facilitates the channeling of energy and concentration. It nevertheless requires a minimum of training to improve the elasticity of the joints—knees, ankles, and pelvis.

- Place your hands upon your thighs, with the palms turned towards the sky (see figure 64).
- Breathe deeply using the Breathing of the Ocean.
- Make use of an exhalation to relax your face and throat. Let the relaxation descend throughout your entire body, even as far as the floor, as though the energy was only passing through you like a conducting wire. This is the intermediary energy that strengthens the forces in order to transmit forms.
- After a few minutes, focus your gaze on the centers of your hands and relax them fully. Feel peace and relaxation settling into you. Even your mental body starts to follow the path of tranquility in readiness. Take advantage of this moment to follow and tame it.
- Exhaling naturally facilitates the relaxation of your physical body, as well as the relaxation and tranquility of the mental body. For that reason, close your eyes at the very beginning of an exhalation. Relax your eyes and direct them downward, in order to see the breath coming out of your

nostrils. Remain attentive to your body. Caress it with your breath. Transmit all your love to it through your breathing.

• At the end of each exhalation, imagine you see the centers of your hands, that you can feel them.

• During the suspension of breath, while your lungs are empty, imagine you are continuing to send breath to your hands in order to relax them further and focus the mental body.

• During the slow, deep inhalation that follows, watch the breath penetrate your nostrils. You should see it and feel it transforming your body.

• At the end of each inhalation, let your mental body pursue the movement as if it were continuous.

Your mental body will manifest itself by the awakening of your senses, which are forms of your physical body. Make use of this instant to follow your mental body more intensely and enter into the dance that occurs during the meeting. Train yourself to focus the mental body on the regularity of the breathing movements. Each pause will give you the opportunity to receive the echo of your body's vibrations. Embrace them with love.

After a few sessions, you will feel new sensations developing in your body in a peaceful fluctuation. In time with your slowed heartbeats, visualize a breeze and waves carrying you away on a breath. For the first time, you have discovered a vital space of your physical body by the manifestation of your mental body, which can only present itself to you through the physical.

Keep your hands opened wide, either as part of a posture or in prayer. They symbolize humility, devotion, acceptance, mercy, and the willingness to learn. This says to your own bodies and to God, "I am opening myself to you. I lay myself in your hands so that you can help me find the link, the path of understanding, forgiveness, and eternal riches."

Since your physical body has radar, this simple position allows it to feel what you expect of it. You will feel goodness and sensitivity. Unfortunately, we often confuse these with sadness and weakness.

After a few months of work, your physical body will begin to confide in you. It wants to tell you, "I am well, I am free, and beauty shines in me." Each day after your session, you will feel your body bathing in the great river of serenity. The way you gaze on the world will have changed. In your eyes, others will perceive the goodness within you that smiles at life. Even your words will leave no room for judgment, because your body emits only tolerance.

Your posture has become familiar to you, and you have finally adopted it as your own. From the moment you place your body in its posture, it frees itself and becomes comfortable. Sometimes, it creates more comfort to place a cushion beneath your buttocks to straighten them and obtain a better spinal alignment. The further you advance in your seeking, the more will take care of the well-being and comfort of the body. You should always respect it in order to appreciate it and appreciate it in order to protect it. Each posture should facilitate the natural slowing of the blood's circulation, pressure, and heart rate, with the goal of approaching a state of tranquility. Always avoid adopting a posture too quickly, without a long preparation with the *asanas*. The daily training with the asanas is aimed precisely at improving the elasticity of the tissues, developing and strengthening the muscles, and aerating and reviving the joints. Your body must recover, in whole or in part, the ease of movement it enjoyed in its younger years.

THE NEXT STEP

Start by settling yourself into your posture. With humility and mercy, let serenity reign within your body as you seek your mental stability.

Place your hands on your thighs and perform the Breathing of the Ocean to obtain mental stability through humility. During the exhalation, and without any contraction, slowly open your eyes.

Create the Mudra of the Energy Link (see figure 39) to better channel your energies and draw closer to your mental body. In this mudra, the thumb and the index finger touch without pressing each another. The palm of the hand forms a plateau on which sits a pyramid, the center of energy. It serves as both a detector and an emitter: You will use it to focus and stock energy. The other fingers point naturally upwards and are relaxed.

To visualize the Mudra of the Energy Link, imagine the breath passing through the circle formed by the thumb and the index finger with each inhalation. The breath will accumulate in the pyramid at the center of the hand. Each exhalation will serve to relax the body and feel the energy in the hand. At the very start of an exhalation, slowly close your eyes, which signifies that you have the image of your mudra engraved sufficiently within you so it intermingles with the sensations of your physical body.

Since the Breathing of the Ocean is no longer adapted to your level of evolution, begin the Breathing of the Yogi. This will permit you to find the different dimensions within your body's state quickly. The Breathing of the Yogi is achieved with several pauses during inhalation: Inhale for two seconds, pause for two seconds, inhale for two seconds, pause for two seconds, and inhale for two seconds. Pausing with your lungs filled should last six seconds. It is imperative that you train sufficiently to increase your respiratory capacity because your body should in no way be distracted in your seeking. If you let impatience overcome you, it is possible to "cheat" with the breathing. But the results will be less satisfactory. Exhalation is carried out slowly, without you worrying about its duration.

- Focus inwardly upon the energy deposited in your hands.
- Inhale for two seconds.
- As you gaze upon your palms, raise your arms.
- Then stop your breathing for two seconds. Your energy will continue on its path. Gaze on it and feel it envelope and

penetrate your physical body.

• Inhale for two more seconds, during which your energy will become more noticeable and almost visible in the sensations of your physical body.

• Pause. During the pause, your energy will slow its movement, but your body will continue to transform itself. A sensation of prickling or numbness may occur, but don't try to develop or translate your feelings.

• During the third inhalation, let the energy rise within the highest part of your body. (Each inhalation allows you to shape the energy of your breath in order to find your existence in its movements.)

• When you pause your breath, your physical body will continue its transformation. During the pause, observe your energy as it leaves your body from the back of the upper neck.

• Throughout your next exhalation, watch the energy leave your body and rise above it. Listen to the echo of your body's vibrations, and with your inner gaze, receive what the eyes could never transmit to you.

The top of the breath should be at the rear of the throat, as in the Breathing of the Ocean. Energy that will nourish your physical body and clothe your mental body is placed in the mudra you have visualized at the centers of your hands. Make use of this energy so that your physical body is active, and your mental body can present you with the colors that reveal its form. Each space in your breathing plays a central role. Apply yourself to this.

The breathing of your body should continue in the same fashion, under your control, but liberated. The dialogue of love has started, because it breathes the energy that activates its life. Breathe the echoes of its vibrations as it surrenders itself to you. You advance further and further along the path of images.

You attract the mental body, and it approaches you, but you don't recognize it at first. You receive circles of light and color that come to you and enter your center. At the same time, you watch the energy leaving from the back of your neck. You observe that your body as it slowly tilts backward like a child falling asleep. The circles of colors and lights group together and become more intense, as though dressing or protecting the child. In reality, they are not coming to you, but you are moving toward them as you take on the forms of the mental body.

You have been watching the energy leave your physical body. You are separating yourself from palpable form to become time.

The mental body will present itself to you in its crudest form before disrobing and offering you its colors, like a flower that offers its soul to a delicate visitor. At the moment of its meeting with the mental body, you tip over into a black space. It will feel like nothingness, the void, as if the ground had abruptly vanished beneath the weight of your body. The world will disappear. You will plunge in a sudden free fall. You will no longer see anything, but you will continue gazing. You will no longer be able to hear anything. But you are in each form; you can hear your senses. You are moving toward the inner world. Although you remain beside your physical body, it no longer represents the same thing. You will understand that you can no longer see it. But you will gaze inwardly and breathe it, as though your breath were the arms of love that stretch out their protecting hands and transmit the affection born of love.

You have just accomplished a great journey to the inner world. Your mental body has become very accessible and quite pleasant. But contrary to what you might believe, it is not over yet. You have entered its most delicate phase—the return. You must come home to your house without destroying the walls—not injuring the flesh.

You may often want to remain in the inner world for as long as possible, because well-being becomes a beauty that is experienced. Life's problems do not exist there.

However, you should never stay more than three minutes outside your physical house, especially at the beginning. Your body needs time to settle comfortably into a routine. You will always find yourself above your body, whether it's located on your right, your left, or in front of you.

In the beginning of your journey, your inhalation and its pause will serve as the motor for leaving the body. You will be floating in a dance guided by the melody of breath. This will assure the link between the physical and mental bodies and your self.

For your return, exhalation will be your driving force. In the same way, you return to your physical body. Each exhalation will take on vital importance. The pauses in exhalation will allow you to listen to your sensations and be attentive, so that during the exhalation you can descend and melt into your body. Through exhalation, you enter into the body and start to perceive the forehead changing shape, as well as sensations of hot and cold. Continue to make use of each exhalation to settle fully into your home. For a short instant, your body will begin to feel as if were burning, then cold will pass over and within it, before it stabilizes.

You have succeeded. You are back within this wonderful body, and from now on, you will see it differently.

There is more. Keep your eyes closed. Inhalation will become your motor for a second time. Make use of your inhalations and their pauses to travel across the pattern of the body. Become conscious of the state of your body. Direct your mental body to the extremities of your hands and feet.

Then "rise" through your entire body. The pauses are ideal for listening, being attentive, and feeling. Take big, free breaths to stretch your body.

The first time I carried out this experiment was during the eighth year of my life. Very often, my father spoke to me about his meetings in the inner world. He invented stories that fascinated me and made me want to experience the same thing. I had the impression that he was thinking out loud, leading me by the hand inside a picture he was painting with the colors and curves of his words. He was gazing into existence, and I listened to his gaze, far from the outside world.

Each day, I told him insistently of my desire to make this journey to meet my self, to leave my physical body without abandoning it. I wanted to journey into my inner space and use my inward gaze to touch what lay within me, although my father believed my body still needed preparation, and I lacked knowledge.

"Little Pyell, I want to teach you to learn, so that you can give to your body what I am giving you—time," he said. "The time to appreciate your consideration towards your body. So that the love it receives from you builds within it the confidence that gives strength. Always give your body time, and it will take it. With the thread of patience it acquires, it will weave the its robe of protection."

Even today, I can still see the stubborn little boy who never gave up. Finally, to my greatest joy, my father made the decision to guide me on the great journey to the inner world. He later confessed he had decided to teach me about my two bodies long before. But first, he stirred me up to want it and helped me to avoid confusing simple wanting with real desire. My father said to me, "You should consider your life like a tree that will provide you with fruit each day. I want to teach you to become a good gardener."

Now, after years of practice and seeking, I am in turn making the decision to teach you. I want to give you enough so that you will be able to meet yourself and become a good gardener. I want to help you obtain the best out of life.

I have just described a simple and accessible method for

you to meet with your mental body. You can and will succeed if you want this. But don't try to go beyond the mental body. There are dangers. Also, as a reminder, don't remain outside your house for more than three minutes. Never forget that the space between here and the inner world is very short. *But the path to travel is very long.*

A BETTER DAILY LIFE

Don't content yourself with performing casual gymnastics. Learn about your bodies so that they will no longer suffer or be ill. Take the path to a better life. Consider your physical body as a child that you love—your child. Don't cry with it over the hurt that tears its flesh but behave like a father and take away its misery.

Draw from within you the wisdom that is born of knowledge. The experience of its life has always made available to you what you need. Never take upon yourself the hurt that makes your body cry. If you want to help your body erase the hurt, don't commit the error of wanting to treat the cause without knowing the reason. Such aggression provokes automatic reactions of self-defense when the cause of harm is not understood. Protect your bodies and no longer leave them alone with their automatic self-defense systems. Look for the circumstances in life that have become the reason.

Apply these teachings to your daily life. Give your bodies the breath of a better life, the breath of love. If your stomach aches, stop saying, "I have a stomachache," because it is only

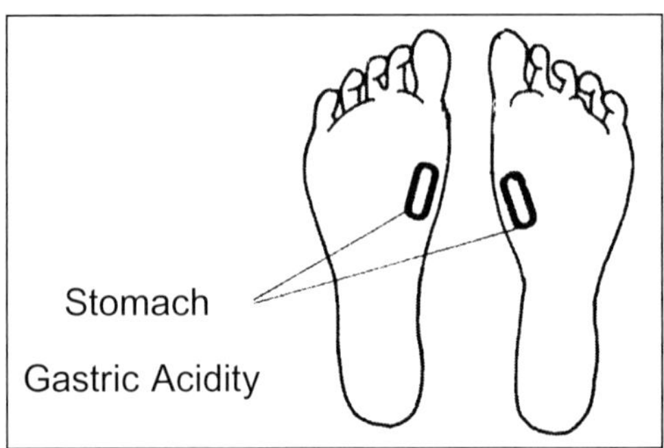

Diagram 1

a part of one of your bodies that hurts. Seek the reason in order to understand the cause (the reactions).

Perform the Asana of the Beneficent Ocean (see figure 37). Practice in small sessions lasting about three minutes. Two or three times in the same day, and at the end of each session, stretch your torso while tilting the pelvis forward. Never forget that any stretching is only really effective on the condition it be performed with deep inhalation.

For quicker results, you can stimulate your digestive tract by means of *digitopuncture*. This is a technique that uses the pressure made with the fingers on specific points located along the meridian lines. This technique makes it possible to stimulate and/or alleviate the flow of vital energy in the body as outlined below.

- Sit down and put your right foot between your hands.
- Place the palms of your hands on the sides of foot, with your fingers placed in the center (metatarsal region).
- Press down with your fingertips to smooth the bottom of your foot.

• Put the fingers of your right hand upon the center indicated for the lungs, heart, and solar plexus (see diagram 2).

• The fingers of your left hand should be applied to the center for the stomach (see diagram 1).

• Start the Breathing of the Ocean.

• During your inhalations, drum strongly on the sole of the foot with the fingertips at the points indicated.

• When you pause with your lungs filled, stop the tapping of your fingers while maintaining the pressure with your hands and smoothing the bottom of the foot.

• Upon exhalation, tap the center of your stomach with the left hand only (see diagram 1).

To do this well, count out at least ten taps for each movement of breathing, according to your respiratory capacity. After two or three breaths, straighten your torso, belch out any excess gas, and start on the other side.

Benefits of Digitopuncture

This exercise helps with gastric acidity, excess gas, constipation, and digestive difficulties.

AVOIDING FATIGUE

You should always protect your physical body. Do so in a way that ensures a healthy life. Perhaps you don't know it, but when your physical body hurts, it complains to the mental body like a child in search of love and protection. The mental body, always present and attentive, builds morale for it in an effort to support it. However, a morale built on a lack of well-

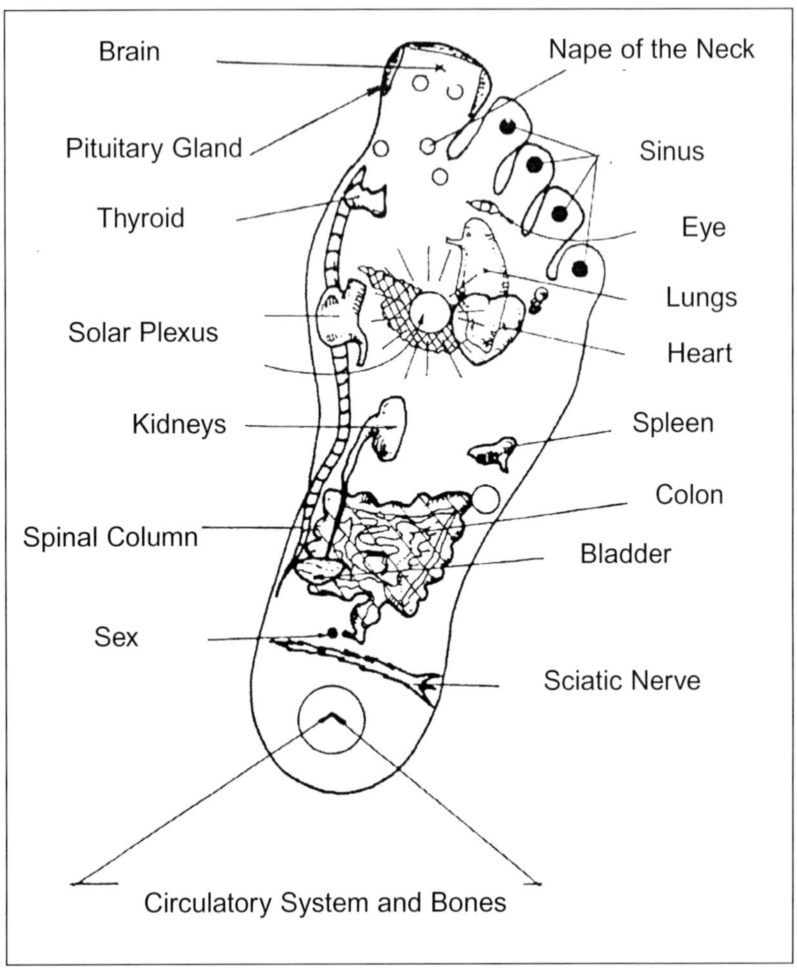

Diagram 2

being is too often negative. *In your emotional life, don't be fooled by love. Your physical body is often hungry, thirsty, and enjoying love. But you need to learn to give love.* The suffering of the physical body may become even greater, to the point

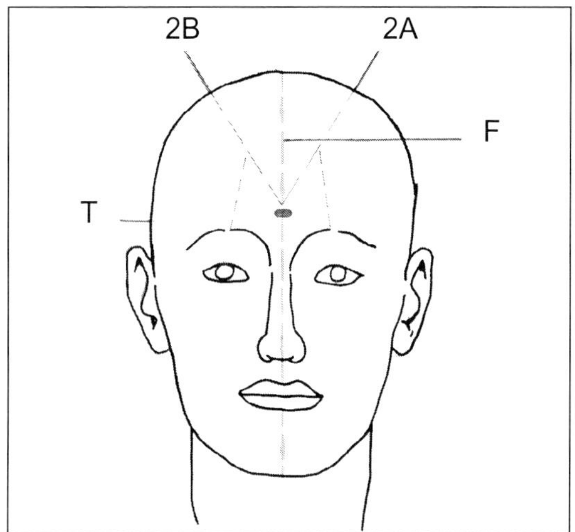

Diagram 3

that you end up exhausting your morale.

Organize yourself so that your physical body is never exhausted. Otherwise, your morale will never be reliable, and your mental body may even begin to decline. You will suffer a general fatigue. Treat fatigue as if it were a relative you are trying to avoid. However, when he or she barges into your life like a rude person, don't treat them like an enemy but like a friend who comes to warn you that the energy of your physical body is not in balance and that your morale is in a state of conflict.

A simplified digitopuncture technique using "facial line circles" will help you relieve your body's fatigue in record time. As a beginner, however you will only obtain results for a few hours.

• Sit down with the soles of your feet flat on the floor.

• Start the Breathing of the Ocean.

• At the same time, bend your arms and put your thumbs, up to the first knuckles, on the temporal muscles (see diagram 3, point T).

• The tips of the other fingers should be placed on either side of the top of your head (see diagram 3, points 2A and 2B) in the line of the reflective zone. To give you more precise benchmarks, the space between the thumb and other fingers is about four fingers wide. The distance between your two hands at the top of the head is about the same. The placements of the thumbs are only indications. When you think you have found the reflective lines, the thumbs will no longer be useful.

• Put pressure on your head with our fingertips.

• As you start to inhale, trace little circles with tapping beats during each loop, in order to push your scalp towards the middle of your head. With each loop, the fingers should get nearer to your forehead by about a quarter-inch.

• When your two hands meet at the top of your forehead, keep applying pressure with your fingertips and flatten all of your fingers against the top of your forehead. The adjacent little fingers should be pushing against one another.

• Keep this position while pausing with your lungs full.

• Before you exhale, relax the back of your neck and let your hands fall. Release your shoulders so that your body relaxes.

• Once you have completed this, exhale freely without

restraint, as if you were holding an object that falls when you open your hands delicately.

- During exhalation, lower your head and release the back of your neck more to stretch the cervical vertebrae and further relax your body.
- At the end of the next pause, with your lungs empty, straighten your head.
- Resume the process with a long, deep inhalation. Keep your fingers on your head.

When your fingers are extended across your upper forehead, they should be located within an inverted pyramid. The line running through point “F” at the center (see diagram 3) will be the border demarcating the placement of the fingers. You should continue pressing until the suspension of breath is over. The little circles with beats should be traced from below to above and move forward. During each inhalation, the average number of beats should be about ten. The pauses in breathing should last from two to four seconds. You will establish the length of your sessions according to your needs; five to ten minutes is enough.

However, be careful, because once you start your digitopuncture sessions, you will experience new sensations that are sometimes awkward. The first exhalations may generate a sense of liberation for you and of pressure in your head, like a bottle of sparkling water that has just been opened. You will also feel a sensation of gravity that will invade your body from head to toe. Your face will fall, giving you the appearance of a person who is just waking up. In short, the first minute will seem like you have been drained of all your energy. Don't practice this if you are about to drive a car, because after the session, you will suffer a loss of reflexes.

Within five minutes, however, your face will look younger and rested. You will have a more open mind and a fresh outlook. Your body will be emptied of nervous tension. Its energies will be reorganized, and your physical body toned, but with a sensation of peace.

Carry out this digitopuncture session each time fatigue takes hold in your body. Grant your body a five-minute session per day, for ten days, to derive great benefit from the exercise. Alternatively, try ten minutes every other day for fifteen days. You will gain in terms of quality of life, and your body will appreciate it.

If you can combine digitopuncture with the asanas I mentioned earlier, then your joy can only grow. The life of your body will be better, and a glow will emerge from within you. Your face will emanate the pleasure of being free.

To avoid fatigue, always remain attentive to your body, and you will be forewarned. Give your body the means of recharging itself with energy. Within it, peace will reign and you will harvest serenity. Every evening, prepare for a regenerative sleep so that your body no longer becomes fatigued. Perform the Asana of Catalepsy to oxygenate and revive your muscles. Also perform the Asana of Delirious Stretching to suppress aches, back pains, persistent contractions, and all nervous and muscular tensions (see figures 27 and 28). However, your body will also need the Asana of Sleep to prepare it for cycles of deep, refreshing sleep. If you put this way of life into practice, your body will find sleep once again. It will be quick in arriving, deep and without agitation.

In a forthcoming book, I will expand on many of the subjects introduced in this work: the education, knowledge, and meeting with the mental body, how to maintain the spinal column in order to stop suffering from backaches, and how to regain suppleness and keep it for good. I will also come back to one of humanity's greatest treasures, if not its greatest: love. I will discuss aspects of sexuality such as how to make love without ejaculating and how to trigger an orgasm at will. I will also explore the capacities of the physical body so that your body also operates at its best.

I would like so much for you to apply yourself to this in each day of your life. Apply yourself to seeing through what you hear; it is one of the best ways to learn to listen.

I send you the Sun.

GLOSSARY

Abductor–*An abductor is any muscle used to pull a body part away from its midline. For example, the abductor muscles of the legs spread the legs away from the midline and away from one another.*

Asana–*In Sanskrit, asana means posture. This word is often used to mean yoga posture specifically, as in such titles as "The Asana of Liberation," "Trikonasana," "Pachimotanasana," etc.*

Biceps–*Biceps are any muscles having two origins. However, the term is usually applied to a flexor in the arm and to another in the thigh.*

Catalepsy–*Catalepsy (also spelled katalepsy) refers to a seizure or attack of fitfulness. In* Breathing Life, *the Yogi presents asanas to PREVENT catalepsy.*

Cervical spine–*The cervical spine is made up of the first seven vertebrae in the spine. It starts just below the skull and ends at the top of the thoracic spine (see below). The cervical spine has a backward "C" shape (lordotic curve) and is much more mobile than either of the thoracic or lumbar regions of the spine. Unlike the other regions of the spine, the cervical spine has special openings in each vertebrae for the arteries that carry blood to the brain.*

Dorsal column–*The dorsal column is the main sensory tract to the brain.*

Elevator muscles–*These are muscles that raise any depressed portion of a bone.*

Kata–*Kata means "down" in Greek. In yoga, the term refers to any movement or practice that takes us deep within.*

Kung-du-yoga–*This is a form of yoga the Yogi has created. It is roughly translated as a flowing yoga, in which everything is one long movement governed by the breath.*

Loincloth of light–*This is one of two loincloths used in pranayama practice. It is the narrower of the two and should measure three yards long and one foot wide.*

Lumbar spine–*The lumbar region is the lower part of the spine between the thoracic region and the sacrum. The lumbar spine consists of five vertebrae. These are the five movable spinal segments of the lower back and largest of the spinal segments.*

Mental body–*This term refers to the invisible or intuitive part of ourselves that absorbs and interprets the world and its images WITHOUT intellectual thinking. If you see a hummingbird flying past and you instantly sense it is giving you a message, then that's your mental body picking up that form of intelligence. We are far more perceptive and present when we consciously engage our mental bodies in our lives.*

Mudra–*A mudra is a specific positioning of the hands and body that is intended to seal the life energy inside the body. Often, a mudra seals off the body's orifices (eyes, ears, mouth, etc.) as well. Mudras are used to increase concentration and hold power within the body during the preparation or close of meditation and yoga sessions.*

Prana–*This prefix means "flow of life."*

Pranayama–*Pranayama is the art and science of yogic breathing. Like many other ancient Indian arts, this science of yogic breathing was almost completely unknown to the average practitioner until recently. However, these techniques have been practiced for generations by serious yoga students worldwide.*

Samadhi–*The first phase of concentration is a state of being aware of one's existence without thinking.*

Seeker's loincloth–*The seeker's loincloth is a piece of cotton or silk cloth, two yards long and one yard wide.*

Viscera–*This term refers to any of the large interior organs in any one of the three great cavities of the body, especially in the abdomen.*